D1180402

COWGIRLS
COCKROACHES
AND
CELEBRITY
LINGERIE

COWGIRLS
COCKROACHES
AND
CELEBRITY
LINGERIE

THE WORLD'S
MOST UNUSUAL
MUSEUMS

Michelle Lovric

ICON BOOKS

Published in the UK in 2007 by
Icon Books Ltd, The Old Dairy, Brook Road,
Thriplow, Cambridge SG8 7RG
email: info@iconbooks.co.uk
www.iconbooks.co.uk

Sold in the UK, Europe, South Africa and Asia
by Faber & Faber Ltd, 3 Queen Square,
London WC1N 3AU or their agents

Distributed in the UK, Europe, South Africa and Asia
by TBS Ltd, TBS Distribution Centre, Colchester Road
Frating Green, Colchester CO7 7DW

This edition published in Australia in 2007
by Allen & Unwin Pty Ltd, PO Box 8500,
83 Alexander Street, Crows Nest, NSW 2065

Distributed in Canada by Penguin Books Canada,
90 Eglinton Avenue East, Suite 700,
Toronto, Ontario M4P 2YE

ISBN: 978-1840468-33-5

Text copyright © 2007 Michelle Lovric

The author has asserted her moral rights.

No part of this book may be reproduced in any form, or by any
means, without prior permission in writing from the publisher.

Every effort has been made to trace the copyright holders of the
copyright material in this book. The author gratefully acknowledges
permission to reprint extracts from the following works: Helen Keller,
The Story of My Life, chapter XXI, 1903, courtesy of the Helen Keller
Archives, American Foundation for the Blind; Pablo Neruda, 'To La
Sebastiana', reprinted by permission of Agencia Literaria Carmen Balcells.

Typeset in 11 on 15.5pt Minion by Wayzgoose

Printed and bound in the UK by
J.H. Haynes & Co. Ltd.

Contents

CONTENTS

Introduction

Strange creatures, human beings. They get passionate about the strangest things, too. All over the world and throughout the ages, people have accumulated extraordinary and extraordinarily diverse objects. In time, some of these collections have grown into museums.

This book offers a worldwide armchair pilgrimage to some of the most interesting museums that can be visited in person or online.

What is a museum? Simply, it's a collection of things, arranged according to someone's idea of order. Within that definition fit any number of institutions: historical, modern, virtual and mythical. Noah's Ark, with its pairs of every creature, was possibly the world's very first museum.

One man's rubbish is another man's relic. No subject, it seems, is too small or strange to have a whole museum devoted to it: asparagus, lawnmowers, ships in bottles, the pets of American presidents, menstruation, worry beads, burnt food.

The museums themselves come in all shapes and sizes. There's the vast SPAM Museum in Minnesota, the tiny Carrot Museum in Belgium, the elegant Phallological Museum in Iceland, the hi-tech Parasitological Museum in Japan, and the chilling Museum of Madness in the old Napoleonic asylum on an island in the Venetian lagoon.

Indeed, if it's atmosphere you crave, you can even stay overnight at the Lizzie Borden Bed & Breakfast, sleeping in the room where Ms Borden was alleged to have given her stepmother the famous '40 whacks' with her axe. Or you can visit the actual scene of many unanaesthetised amputations at the Old Operating Theatre in London. It has hardly changed at all.

There's a historical pedigree for even these unusual collections. Medieval churches were in their way early museums. No church worth its salt lacked a little piece of a saint or a natural wonder (like an ostrich egg or fragment of meteorite) to inspire its worshippers, and encourage new ones to visit.

The quest for the curious soon became secular. Collectors all over Europe began to create strange rooms of colourful stuffed or bottled creatures, arranged in poses like the extras in the finale of a Broadway musical. Most famous was the museum owned by the fabulously named Ole Worm, a Danish professor of medicine (1588–1654). Domestic mini-museums became all the rage. From the late 17th century, every fashionable family had a little glass-topped box on a stand in which it displayed exotic items collected from around the world. This 'cabinet of curiosities' became an obsession for some, and from them small museums grew.

At this point, collections forked off into one of two evolutionary destinies. Some turned into serious, grown-up museums, national institutions, or were donated to them. These are the Big Beasts among museums: venerable, authoritative, grand. Some might even describe them as a little pompous. This is the kind of museum anathematised by G.K. Chesterton in his 1931 essay 'On Sightseeing': 'The Museum is not meant for the wanderer to see by accident or for the pilgrim to see with awe. It is meant for the mere slave of a routine of self-education to stuff himself with every sort of incongruous intellectual food in one indigestible meal ...'

The American writer Nathaniel Hawthorne, writing in 1856, saw them as something to be struggled through: 'Yesterday I visited the British Museum; an exceedingly tiresome affair. It quite crushes a person to see so much at once; and I wandered from hall to hall with a weary and heavy heart.'

Fortunately, other museums chose the road less travelled. They have stayed small, eclectic, fascinating and endearing. Unlike the great national museums, these small collections, often in private ownership, have never really been accountable to anyone. Their curatorial opinions have remained their own business. There are few more pleasurable experiences for the visitor than finding an outrageous piece of curatorial folly in such places. Mark Twain joyfully recorded a museum in Havana where 'there are two skulls of Christopher Columbus – one when he was a boy and one when he was a man'.

In America, 'Dime Museums' provided garish entertainment for the curious masses. They offered a mixture of live freaks and preserved specimens. Like all small museums they had to fight for the public's attention – and their dimes. The great showman P.T. Barnum, writing in *The Nation*, 10 August 1865, shrugged off those who sneered at his displays: 'I am not thin-skinned, and I know my Museum was not so refined or classic or scientifically arranged as the foreign governmental institutions, for mine had to support my family, while those require annually from the government thousands of pounds ... [T]o make it self-supporting, I was obliged to popularize it, and while I still held on to the "millions of curiosities," millions of people were only induced to see them because, at the same time, they could see whales, giants, dwarfs, Albinoes, dog shows, *et cetera*.'

There's another difference between the great museums and the small ones. Once only the rich could afford a private collection. Both the collecting and displaying of unusual objects were luxuries. This meant that what ended up in the so-called serious museums were the things that wealthy people liked, and could purchase or donate (thereby immortalising their own names): antiquities, art, costly jewels and serious scientific objects. The American writer Lewis H. Lapham claimed that he could never pass by the Metropolitan Museum of Art in New York 'without thinking of it not as a gallery of living portraits but as a cemetery of tax-deductible wealth'.

No longer is that the case. It doesn't take a great deal of money to collect fortune cookies, frogs or statistics about rampant consumerism. Many people, in the first world at least, are affluent enough to personally collect whatever appeals to them, and have the leisure time to do it. There's no need for a vast mausoleum built at vaster cost. Any small building will serve – the curator's own home, an electricity substation, a converted ladies' lavatory. Or a factory: some companies, like the producers of humble household names such as Jell-O and SPAM, have acquired so many interesting artefacts in the course of their commercial history that they are now opening fascinating museums of their own.

Edmond de Goncourt claimed that a picture in a museum heard more nonsense than anything else in the world. No one could accuse the museums in this book of pompousness. There's simply no possibility of or room for pretentiousness, either in the visitor or the exhibits, unless the curating is done with *intentional* irony, as at the Museum of Jurassic Technology.

And now there's a brave new world of possibility for museums: the internet. Where no one is accountable, and anything can be posted. A simple digital camera and a domain name will serve where bricks-and-mortar and shelving were once obligatory. The internet means that almost anyone can post a museum online and share their obsession and their collection with the world.

Someone should curate the curators of small museums; make a little museum about them, virtual or visitable. A visit to the museums in the book is a visit to another side of human nature. The curators are all marked by their devotion to their subject, their sheer single-mindedness, the depth of their knowledge. But their curatorial personalities differ vastly: some are quiet and modest, while others are extrovert and larger than life.

People who visit these small museums, online or in person, may have the privilege of getting to know personally the people who set them up. Most keepers of private museums thrive on the wonder and interest of their visitors – they need encouraging, so please visit. And if you can't visit, please email to tell them if the website gave you pleasure! Please write! Many, if not most, small museums struggle on without public funding, surviving only on the unlimited dedication of their owners.

The museum addresses and exhibits listed here were current at the time of writing and verified with the curators themselves insofar as possible. It's the nature of small museums that they are very vulnerable to change. Increasingly stringent health-and-safety regulations have forced many private museums, those once kept in basements and front rooms of private houses, to close their doors to the public and go online. Sometimes high rents force these little museums out of business altogether … hence, for example, a sad farewell in 2005 to Johnny Fox's Freakatorium in New York City, a weird museum about weird museums.

Some displaced museums appeal on their websites for offers of public display space – and some of these pleas, it's to be hoped, will have been met by the time this book is published. Has anyone got a good home for a Potato Museum or the Museum of Menstruation? If so, please contact the curators at the websites listed in this book.

It's a wretched fact of life that many specialist museums do not survive the deaths of their loving owners. Among others, Kathleen Mann's exquisite little Cat Museum in Harrow-on-the-Hill is sadly missed. The passing of the redoubtable Elizabeth Tashijan in January 2007 meant the certain end of her once-famous Nut Museum in Old Lyme, Connecticut. And the death of Rosemary Wells, the world's leading authority on the Tooth Fairy, saw the closing of her Tooth Fairy Museum in Deerfield, Illinois.

In some heartening cases, like the Bottle-Peter Museum in Ærø, Denmark, and the Mary and Marvin Johnson Gourd Museum in North Carolina, USA, friends and family have kept the museums going.

The author will be very happy to hear of any updates for subsequent editions.

Now, a word on the selection of museums in this book. There are about 41,000 museums in 194 countries of the world. How to narrow that down to a mere 80? The brief was 'most unusual'. 'Weird' is a route that has been travelled by several excellent museum books before this one, and there are only so many times the reader will be diverted by descriptions of Bimbo Boxes and two-headed rattlesnakes in one book. There are some museums that must be common to all such books – they are simply too interesting to ignore. America's bizarre roadside museums are part of folk history and deservedly have their own guidebooks devoted to them. But in this book we have taken the whole world, actual and virtual, as our territory, so there are museums in Chile, Malaysia and Poland alongside their bigger American brothers, and some internet sites that give a whole new interpretation to the concept of a museum.

We have also tried to look at museums that haven't received so much attention to date. This isn't because they aren't marvellous, but simply because they have opened only in recent years, like the Museum of Madness in Venice or the Spy Museum in Washington. Others are situated in places not so often mentioned in the annals of tourism ... such as the Iceman Museum in Bolzano and the Bagpipe Museum in Morpeth.

'Unusual' is a big brief. Any subject could be explored. The reader may ask why sex museums aren't specifically visited in this book. The answer is simple. Sex isn't strange. Museums of sex tend to cross the borderline from 'strange' to prurient. That's not really so interesting. And sex museums don't appear to have a broad appeal. The Museum of Eroticism in Venice recently closed down after a brief existence. The nearest we have come to a sex museum are the excellent Museum of Menstruation, a classic of its kind and one of the most interesting and erudite sites on the web, and the aforementioned admirable Icelandic Phallological Museum. (Perhaps museums about sex are redundant anyway. As the French anthropologist Michel Leiris observed: 'Nothing seems more like a whorehouse to me than a museum. In it you find the same equivocal aspect, the same frozen quality.')

Another important point: no one has paid for their inclusion in this book. It was sad to note during research that some museums, when approached, declined to give information. It was only later that it became apparent that they had been conditioned by current market trends to jump to the conclusion that a fee would be payable for an entry. Others even volunteered payment, assuming that it would be necessary. Such times we live in! When we sent out a second letter, explaining that this was a *proper* book, with a good publishing house, and that no payment was required, well, then we were happily deluged with enthusiastic help.

Opening times aren't listed in this book because they are subject to such frequent change and also at the mercy of local public holidays, and, in the case of the very tiny museums, the vagaries of the babysitter and the dog-walker. Therefore phone numbers and website coordinates are given. If you plan a visit to any of the museums cited in the book, we urge you to check with the museum before setting out in order to avoid disappointment. Small museums sometimes open by appointment only, or just a few days a month. Similarly, we decided not to list admission charges as these are frequently altered.

We have, though, mentioned museum shops where they are interesting, and especially where merchandise is available online and therefore even to people with no hope of visiting the actual museum. Les Jones, a witty internet blogger (www.lesjones.com) insists that the most popular features of any museum are the gift shop and the restrooms, and that someone ought to do a museum of gift shops and restrooms.

While we would not go so far as that, it's true that museum shopping is a highly enjoyable pastime and deserves to be recognised as such. Moreover, gift-shop proceeds go to support the many museums that operate on a shoestring and their curators' tireless enthusiasm alone, and therefore deserve all the help that they can get. Plus, where else but at the Museum of Jurassic Technology would you be able to buy 'the Horn of Mary Davis' reproduced as a candle and candleholder? Or a T-shirt sombrely emblazoned with the Proustian sentiment 'Dispirited after a Dreary Day with the Prospect of a Depressing Morrow'? The covetable fridge magnet showing a pig with machine guns is not readily available outside the House of Terror in Budapest. And if you want to adopt a wolf for your own dog, you'll just have to go online and buy it at the Wolf Song of Alaska museum.

Finally, special and heartfelt thanks to the curators who answered my endless questions in person or by phone, email and letter, and were generous with sending material, photographs, explanations and personal comments. People who were irreproachably patient when asked, 'What exactly does the model elephant say?' and 'Please explain what the Slaughter Festival entails?', or 'Are clowns sinister?', 'Oh, the double-headed rattlesnake died, did he?' and 'Do you think the alien baby looks sad?'

Michelle Lovric
London, September 2007

THE COCKROACH HALL OF FAME

2231-B West 15th Street, Plano, Texas 75075, USA
Telephone: (USA 001) 972 519 0355
www.pestshop.com

'The cockroach and the bird were both here long before we were. Both could get along very well without us, although it is perhaps significant that of the two the cockroach would miss us more.'

Joseph Wood Krutch

The Pest Shop on 15th Street, Plano, Texas might look like just another modest establishment selling products to deal with bugs and rats.

It *is* that, but there's an added attraction here. The owner of the shop, Michael 'Cockroach Dundee' Bohdan, has made something of a fetish of his collection of dead cockroaches. He specialises in *Periplanteta americana*, the all-American cockroach.

Mind you, Mr Bohdan doesn't discriminate interspecially. He insists: 'There isn't a cockroach I don't like, not even a dead one.'

Not just cockroaches. In his book, *What's Buggin' You?*, Mr Bohdan explains the latest techniques for terminating everything from ants to gophers. In the shop, he sells humane live traps for rabbits, rats, raccoons, possums, squirrels, skunks and armadillos. Few squirrels have been known to resist the delights of his special baits, 'Pecan Surprise' and 'Loganberry Delight'.

But Mr Bohdan's heart belongs to cockroaches. Over the years, he has created and curated many miniature dioramas of preserved cockroaches in costume. His Cockroach Hall of Fame was richly endowed with entries in the annual 'Cockroach in Art' competition that he ran for years.

Among his cockroach celebrities are a smiling David Letteroach and a very glitzy Liberoachi in a white mink cape, seated at a white piano with a tiny golden candelabra. This masterpiece was created by an 85-year-old lady from Fort Worth, Texas. Important American icons are also represented: the Statue of Liberty is shown up to her elbow in a cockroach that looks rather like a crunchy oven glove. Marilyn Monroach shimmers in her trademark white dress and Elvis Roachley struts his stuff on more legs than usual. And let's not forget Batroach. Or H. Ross Peroach. One scene is set at the Bates Roach Motel. And there's a spiritually uplifting *Last Supper with Roaches*. Also, a sunny beach scene with windsurfing roaches.

A special platform is always reserved for the latest winner in another competition run by Mr Bohdan – for the biggest roach found dead or alive in America each year. A surprisingly large number of contestants are posted to Plano, in various stages of decomposition.

How big? Big enough. In sailors' parlance, a really big American cockroach is known as a 'Mahogany Mouse'.

If dead cockroaches don't do it for you, live ones are also available. The Cockroach Hall of Fame has its own interactive display of live Madagascar Hissing Roaches that grow to ten centimetres (four inches) in length. How interactive? If you pick one up, it will hiss at you. They also run races.

Mr Bohdan offers one additional service. He will do his best to identify any pest you bring in, free of charge, so long as it's in one piece. The best way to preserve your critters, he explains, is to place them in a jar of rubbing alcohol. He promises: 'In most cases, I will be able to identify your pest with the help of my trusty 30x Stereoscope.'

Mr Bohdan will be happy to let you pose for photos wearing his hat decorated with dead roaches. As he comments: 'It's not the Smithsonian Institute, but the Cockroach Hall of Fame draws people from all over the world.'

The Hunterian Museum

The Royal College of Surgeons,
35–43 Lincoln's Inn Fields, London WC2A 3PE, England
Telephone: (UK 0044) (0)207 869 6560
www.rcseng.ac.uk/museums

'He would set about cutting up the carcass of a whale with the same greatness of gusto that Michael Angelo would have hewn a block of marble.' William Hazlitt on John Hunter

John Hunter (1728–93) was London's great scientific showman: surgeon, dentist, anatomist, pathologist, taxidermist and teacher. This irrepressible Scot also had a taste for the exotic, and is said to have performed the dissection of an Egyptian mummy as an after-dinner entertainment.

A fearless surgeon and an undoubted workaholic, Hunter was also the author of books as diverse as *The Natural History of the Human Teeth* (1771), *Treatise on the Venereal Disease* (1786) and *Directions for Preserving Animals, and Parts of Animals, for Examination* (1785). He was a paragon of unsqueamish Enlightenment curiosity.

It would be hard to find a natural phenomenon that did not interest Hunter: blood circulation, pus formation and the growth of deer antlers were among his studies. In his lifetime, Hunter accrued an incredible collection of diseased human parts preserved in glass jars. To his larder of foetuses, strangulated hernias and ovarian cysts, he added congenital monstrosities of all species, dissected animals and the skeletons of a 40-foot bottlenose whale and the first giraffe seen in England.

An Eskimo who visited in the 1770s not unsurprisingly grew fearful at the sight of so many human bones, asking the guide: 'Are these the bones of Esquimaux whom Mr Hunter has killed and eaten? … Will he eat us and put our bones here?'

Hunter's home in Leicester Square, where he moved in 1783, contained an operating theatre, dissecting room and boilers for rendering down bones. Live specimens included wolves, leopards, jackals and bees.

Hunter's famous collection of bottle specimens was swelled by gifts from other naturalists such as Joseph Banks. By the time of Hunter's death in 1793, the collection was unrivalled anywhere in the world, containing 13,682 specimens, arranged in a highly rational manner for teaching purposes. It was open each May to 'noblemen and aristocrats' and in October to fellow scientists. Other visitors were entertained at Hunter's discretion.

It was discovered on his death that Hunter's passion for collecting had outstripped his means. The collection was sold to the state in 1799 to pay his debts and was immediately placed into the care of the College of Surgeons under a separate Board of Trustees at Lincoln's Inn Fields, where it has remained to this day. The museum reopened in February 2005 after an extensive renovation that has left it gleaming, beautiful and faintly sinister. There's an unearthly fascination at the sight of so much mortality and immortality so obsessively labelled and choreographed.

Its appearance, like a carefully ordered nightmare, offers so much more than Damien Hirst, renowned for his 'shocking' and 'innovative' claim that a dead animal in formaldehyde constitutes real art. The Young British Artist's celebrated shark seems both derivative and crude in comparison with the haunting exhibits in the Hunterian. Indeed, some of the exhibits have inspired plays, poetry and novels, partly for their strange life histories and their shimmering afterlife in the Hunterian Museum.

Among the highlights: Winston Churchill's dentures; paintings by George Stubbs, including one of a rhino exhibited in London in the early 1790s; the brain of Charles Lister Babbage, inventor of the computer; and Joseph Lister's first antiseptic spray, a major breakthrough in the history of surgery.

Two exhibits vie for the award of most pathetic. The first is the lower face of a Victorian match-maker who suffered the dreadful occupational disease known as 'phossy jaw', caused by too much contact with phosphorus. The second and perhaps saddest exhibit is the 2.3-metre (7'7") skeleton of the giant Charles Byrne. All through Byrne's short and wretched life as a freak-show artist, Hunter kept him under morbid observation, much to the giant's distress, finally pouncing on his corpse when he died in London in 1783. Poor Byrne had hoped to be buried at sea, to avoid dissection, but it was not to be.

The Lizzie Borden Bed & Breakfast and Museum

92 Second Street, Fall River, Massachusetts 02721, USA
Telephone: (USA 001) 508 675 7333
www.lizzie-borden.com

> *Lizzie Borden took an axe,*
> *And gave her mother 40 whacks;*
> *When she saw what she had done,*
> *She gave her father 41.*

In 1893, the whole world was convulsed by the sensational trial of Lizzie Borden for the axe-murders of her father and step-mother. More than a hundred years after the vicious crime, Lizzie Borden's hometown has embraced its famous daughter as a tourist attraction. The Fall River Historical Society has created a Lizzie Borden exhibition that includes a graphic account of the crime and various forensic displays from the trial, including the shocking crime-scene photographs; a bedspread and pillow shams spotted with blood; locks of the victims' hair; and two paper tags for 'Mr Borden's stomach' and 'Mrs Borden's stomach'. There's also a bloodstained camisole, 'hairs taken from the hatchet' and a handleless hatchet, said to be the murder weapon itself.

Lizzie enthusiasts can visit the scene of the crime, a hand-some Greek revival house now restored to its former glory. In the gift shop, there are quaint Lizzie Borden hatchet earrings for the ladies. Enthusiasts can even sleep in the house itself: the Lizzie Borden Bed & Breakfast (restored to the 'original look at the time of the murders') offers eight sumptuous bedrooms for guests with strong stomachs, who can sleep (or try to) in the Andrew and Abby Borden Suite, or in the room where Abby was actually murdered. The next morning visitors can buy an 'I Survived the Night' T-shirt at the gift shop.

Manager Lee-ann Wilber enthuses, somewhat scarily: 'Here at Lizzie Borden's we treat everyone like family. Come and axe us anything!'

The website elaborates: 'Apart from that bloody murder all those years ago, our hospitality is impeccable! ... Guests are treated to a breakfast similar to the one the Bordens ate on the morning of the murders, which includes bananas, johnny-cakes, sugar cookies and coffee in addition to a delicious meal of breakfast staples.' The only item omitted from the Bordens' own breakfast is the three-day-old mutton broth.

What could be more romantic? But honeymooners should be warned: at the time of the sensational trial the *New York Times* claimed that nearly 2,000 divorces were occasioned by husbands and wives arguing over the verdict.

Lizzie Borden was cleared of the murders, but her name remains indissolubly associated with the horror of that sizzling August day in 1892 when her father and stepmother were butchered (with 29 whacks, in fact – not the 81 of the famous song, sung eerily in children's voices on the website).

Lizzie's acquittal remains controversial – why, for example, had she tried to buy prussic acid just before the murders, and why was she seen burning a blue dress just afterwards? Relations were strained between Lizzie and her stepmother ... and no one else was ever convicted of the crime.

The online Museum of Menstruation records one fascinating clue – that Lizzie 'had fleas' at the time of the murder, meaning that she was menstrual or premenstrual, an angle still to be fully explored by the forensic scientists.

THE SULABH INTERNATIONAL MUSEUM OF TOILETS

Sulabh Gram, Mahavir Enclave, Palam Dabri Marg,
New Delhi 110 045, India
Telephone: (India 0091) (0)11 2503 1518 / 2503 1519
www.sulabhinternational.org
www.sulabhtoiletmuseum.org

'Toilet is definitely a part of human culture and hence one just cannot shy away from it. Its importance cannot be overemphasised. Its necessity cannot be wished away.'

Dr Bindeshwar Pathak, founder

You may laugh at first, but the reasons behind the founding of this museum are both sobering and staggering. Even today, 110 million Indian houses lack modern toilets. Ten million are serviced only by buckets. The effect on health is disastrous. In the world's developing countries, 1.5 million children under five die each year from diarrhoea caused by lack of sanitation.

Historically, battles have been lost, populations wiped out and epidemics spread because of mistakes and carelessness in the disposal of human waste.

Dr Bindeshwar Pathak's NGO Sulabh International crusades for modern sanitation in India. He argues that not just lives but human dignity are compromised without it. He cites the plight of India's Untouchables, whose occupation it is to collect and dispose of human waste. Girls are denied schooling because of a lack of female facilities. Sulabh International has pioneered the use of cheap and efficient toilets in the underprivileged areas of India, toilets that do not require cleaning by human 'scavengers', and the provision of affordable public facilities. An Indian writer has observed: 'What Abraham Lincoln did for Blacks in America, Dr Pathak has done for scavengers in India. Both are great redeemers.'

Education and research have been key to the NGO's development. Dr Pathak acquired an enormous amount of material in the process. 'The toilet deserves no less attention than the kitchen' is his message. In keeping with his philosophy that human waste should not be treated as a dirty secret but as a challenge for the imagination and technology, he founded the Museum of Toilets in 1990, partly inspired by a visit to Madame Tussaud's in London. His museum houses an extraordinary collection of documents and artefacts detailing the historic evolution of toilets from 2500 BC to modern times. Also chronicled are fascinating social customs and toilet etiquettes through the ages and around the world. The museum is not to be missed on a visit to New Delhi. But much material can be viewed on the excellent website.

The Hindu scripture Vishnu Purana, from 1500 BC, laid down an elaborate code for married people: before relieving themselves, each person was to chant a certain verse and cover their head with a cloth. A sacred thread was to be rolled up and put on the right ear. During the process, silence was to be observed, and the person had to face north during the day and south at night. Many texts lay extraordinary stress on hygiene rituals after defecation. The Vishnu Purana, for example, prescribed that the left hand was to be washed ten times and the right hand seven times, and both feet to be cleaned with earth and water three times. Bachelors and students, the text insisted, should observe the rules 'twice as intensely' as others.

The flush toilet, first invented in the 15th century, soon became an objet d'art. The Museum of Toilets features an outstanding collection of decorative water closets. Highlights: a mobile commode in the shape of a treasure chest, used by Englishmen camping out on hunting trips; a French commode designed to look like a stack of books; beautifully decorated Austrian cisterns from the 19th century; and a replica of the throne-like toilet used by King Louis XIII of France. His successor, Louis XIV, used to give audiences while using a commode under his throne. There's a microwave toilet and an electric toilet used by the US Navy in its submarines.

One of the most interesting and unusual collections is of poems dedicated to toilets and human waste. The greatest bathroom bard of all time was probably French poet Eustorg de Beaulieu in the 16th century, but there are many others who have celebrated faeces and urine with uninhibited relish.

A converted warehouse in Worcester, Massachusetts hosts the American Sanitary Plumbing Museum (39 Piedmont Street, telephone (USA 001) 508 754 9453). This museum includes historical items such as china lavatories and clawfoot baths, and a section of wooden pipe from a water main that supplied the docks where the Boston Tea Party was held.

THE INTERNATIONAL SPY MUSEUM

800 F Street NW, Washington, DC 20004, USA
Telephone: (USA 001) 202 393 7798
www.spymuseum.org

'Use every means in your power to obtain Intelligence from the Enemy.'　　　　　　　　　　　President George Washington

One of the slickest and sneakiest museum websites on the net draws the visitor in with a heart beating extra fast. Before you know it, you've clicked on as a special agent. Your mission (should you choose to accept it): information gathering. Your target: the International Spy Museum. Prepare yourself for a whirlwind of intrigue, danger and sudden 'termination'.

PSSSST. Some 'spookspeak' you'll need to know, to get you through this covert operation alive: Birdwatcher: British Intelligence slang for a spy; Dead Drop: secret location where materials can be left for another party to retrieve; Legend: a spy's fictional background; Swallow: a female agent who seduces (the male of the species is known as a Raven); Throwaway: an expendable agent; Wet Job: an operation that involves killing.

Appropriately enough, this enormous state-of-the-art museum opened in 2002 inside a cluster of late Victorian buildings that once housed the offices of the DC–Baltimore chapter of the American Communist Party. Across the street is the FBI headquarters.

The museum contains the largest collection of espionage objects ever placed on public display: everything from a Russian lipstick pistol to the mighty German Enigma Cipher Machine and the 'escape boots' supplied to British Second World War pilots. (They contained a penknife to trim them down to look like civilian shoes.)

The museum is arranged in sections with names like Covers and Legends, School for Spies, the Briefing Room, Spies Among Us, War of the Spies and Ground Truth.

In the School for Spies section, you can see over 200 Bond-style gadgets, and learn about microdots and invisible ink, buttonhole and wristwatch cameras, bugs and disguise techniques developed by Hollywood artists for the CIA. Interactive displays test the visitor for the innate skills needed to be a successful spy and maintain a convincing cover.

The Secret History of History takes the visitor back to the times of Moses, Elizabeth I, George Washington and Joseph Stalin. This section explains the evolution of secret codes and introduces the Sisterhood of Spies, a select few of the many female agents from the US Civil War through the first decades of the 20th century.

The Second World War was the golden age of spying: never had there been so much double-crossing, code-breaking, bluffing and spy-ringing. The museum explains Ultra, Enigma and the brilliant Navajo code-talkers. Some spies hid their secrets behind a blaze of celebrity, like Oscar-winning director John Ford, sportsman Moe Berg and the chanteuse Josephine Baker who 'ran errands' for de Gaulle. The 20th century's biggest secret – how to make an atom bomb – was stolen from America by a band of Soviet spies.

When the Iron Curtain descended and a Red Scare terrified America, spies were at work even inside their own countries. The

23

exhibition explains the terror of East Germany's intelligence service, the notorious Stasi, the covert operations of spies like Kim Philby and Robert Hanssen, and their eventual detection and exposure.

In June 2007 the museum launched Operation Spy™, a ground-breaking immersive experience. In an action-packed hour, participants role-play US intelligence officers on an international mission to locate a missing nuclear device being sold to a rogue nation.

The Spies on Screen programme shows films with an espionage theme. Virtual visitors can listen to the monthly SpyCast™, featuring interviews with ex-spies, intelligence experts and espionage scholars. Accessible through the museum's homepage, SpyCast™ is hosted by Peter Earnest, executive director of the museum and a former CIA operations officer.

At the Spy City Café (9th and F Streets) visitors can play table-top espionage games while chewing on Spy Dogs. Bestsellers in the 5,000-square-foot (465-square-metre) museum store include the 'Deny Everything' hoodie, rear-view sunglasses and a CD-ROM of 'Music to Spy By'.

THE PROCEEDINGS OF THE ATHANASIUS KIRCHER SOCIETY

Online at www.kirchersociety.org

'The Athanasius Kircher Society was chartered to perpetuate the spirit and sensibilities of the late Athanasius Kircher, SJ. Our interests extend to the wondrous, the curious, the singular, the esoteric, and the sometimes hazy frontier between the plausible and the implausible – anything that Father Kircher might find inspiring if he were alive today.'

Joshua Foer, on the Proceedings website

Believe every word. This splendid online museum combines the best of modern technology and photography with lashings of good old-fashioned curiosity. And the visitor can also 'mingle' with other guests on the site, commenting on the society's postings and the postings of others.

Kircher himself was incurably curious, a designer of devices like the Sunflower Clock. Born in 1602, the German Jesuit scholar was centuries ahead of his time, a kind of late-flowering Da Vinci, a pioneer in microbiology, geology, medicine, music, Chinese and Egyptian studies and the projection of images and encryption.

Until recently, Kircher was popularly known as the chronicler of the infamous 'cat piano', which he describes in his 1650 work *Musurgia Universalis*. 'In order to raise the spirits of an Italian prince burdened by the cares of his position, a musician created for him a cat piano. The musician selected cats whose natural voices were at different pitches and arranged them in cages side by side, so that when a key on the piano was depressed, a mechanism drove a sharp spike into the appropriate cat's tail. The result was a melody of meows that became more vigorous as the cats became more desperate. Who could not help but laugh at such music? Thus was the prince raised from his melancholy.'

The cat piano is, of course, illustrated in the Proceedings site, along with other unusual vehicles powered by animals, including one driven by a fish swimming round a large tank. Musical instruments are a favourite subject, with many marvels portrayed, such as the Great Stalacpipe Organ in Luray Caverns, Virginia, billed as 'the world's largest musical instrument'.

This site works rather like the human brain, branching out in all directions. One thing always leads to a dozen others – an article about a historic shrunken-head collection leads to a posting of shrunken heads for sale on eBay. There's an Australian man who typed the numbers from one to a million – in words. It took him sixteen years ... which leads to the world's longest diary, 35 million words, written by Robert Shields, and enlivened by a tendency to scrapbook personal items such as nasal hair ... which takes us to artist Tom Phillips who attaches his own hair clippings to his sculptures. And Japanese sculptor Hananuma Masakichi, who carved his own likeness out of wood, attaching not just the hair, but the fingernails, teeth and toenails pulled from his own body.

There's a posting on lachrymatory bottles used to store human tears. During the 19th century, some bottles had openings to allow evaporation. When the bottle was dry, the mourning period was deemed over. This calls to mind Thomas Edison's

Last Breath, allegedly captured in a test tube and now kept at the Henry Ford Museum in Dearborn, Michigan.

The society sets itself challenges, like finding the oldest living creature on earth (currently, Harriet, a 175-year-old Galapagos land tortoise, who knew Charles Darwin; though this youngster has only recently inherited the title, after the death of a 255-year-old tortoise named Adwatiya in India). It looks at a disturbing film made in Russian in 1940 about successful resuscitations of dead dogs. And shows Swiss photography of the effect of different hallucinogenic drugs on spiders constructing their webs.

Winner and losers abound. There's a compendium of failed bird-men; of Talmudic mnemonists, who successfully memorised vast tracts of law; of people uselessly obsessed with designing an engine strong enough to lift the whole earth; and a whole section on aquatic ambulism – devices for walking on water.

THE WIELICZKA SALT MINES MUSEUM

10 Daniłowicza Street, 32-020 Wieliczka, near Krakow, Poland
Telephone: (Poland 0048) (0)12 278 7375
www.kopalnia.pl

*'The Saline Works of Wieliczka are not less magnificent than the
Egyptian pyramids, but certainly more useful.'*

'Le Laboureur', French traveller, 1647

Deep in the Polish earth, glittering white chapels, ghostly
human figures, gnomes, chandeliers, winding staircases,
obelisks, ornate Gothic portals ... all painstakingly sculpted
from salt.

The 50-metre-long (164-foot) chapel of St Kinga is a complete church 100 metres (328 feet) underground, including an
ornate altar and scenes from the New Testament. Most of these
marvels were not sculpted by professional artists, but by dedicated, gifted miners who stayed underground after work to craft
them.

Thirteen million years ago this area was covered by a shallow,
salty sea. Tectonic movements left vast salt deposits deep underground. Salt was first mined here at least 1,000 years ago. It was
during the reign of Boleslaus the Chaste in the 13th century that
rock salt was discovered. Boleslaus' bride Kinga was a Hungarian
princess. She received as her dowry a salt mine in Marmaros.
The legend is that she cast her engagement ring down that mine.
The ring, together with salt deposits, miraculously travelled to
Wieliczka. When she arrived in Poland, Kinga ordered the local
miners to dig. In the first block of salt they found her ring.

Kinga, the patroness of miners, was canonised in 1999 by Pope John Paul II.

Before refrigeration and modern chemicals, salt was on a par with today's oil as a vital commodity. It was needed for the preservation of meat, butter and fish, the tanning of hides, and later also for the production of gunpowder. The 'white gold' turned the Polish town of Wieliczka into one of the world's richest centres. A pillar of salt supported the monarchy and the entire economy. Casimir the Great used the income from the salt mines to finance a new university.

Miners first extracted salt by boiling the briny water. Later they dug for rock salt, sinking shafts into the ground. Today a 300-kilometre (186-mile) labyrinth of tunnels connects 3,000 chambers of vast size and haunting beauty. Over the years, millions of tourists have made the subterranean pilgrimage, including Goethe, Balzac, Chopin, Sarah Bernhardt and Emperor Franz Josef. Copernicus is said to have visited the mine in 1493, and a chamber of green salt is named after him. The early tourists were treated to boating on a pea-green brine lake, rides on horse-drawn carts through the passages, and firework displays.

Today's guided tours are on foot, commencing 64 metres (209 feet) underground and finishing 135 metres (443 feet) below in the world's biggest mining museum. There's also a restaurant and a souvenir shop. More recent attractions include a tableau of little salt dwarfs performing mining duties and modern sculptural additions to the chapels.

There's a sombre reason behind the many beautiful chapels. Life down the mines was perilous, with flood, collapse, fire and explosions from methane gas always threatening. So the miners built themselves places to hear mass every morning. These days a sound and light show illustrates for tourists the dreadful dangers that the Wieliczka miners had to confront for centuries. A major flood in 1992 finally closed the working part of the mines.

Because of the extraordinary acoustics of St Kinga (not to mention its suggestive atmosphere and the opulence of its salt-crystal chandeliers) it is sometimes used as a concert venue. There's also a sanatorium for respiratory illnesses. This clinic was established in 1839 by the mine's in-house physician, Feliks Boczkowski, and originally treated 36 illnesses from 'running nose' to infertility, hysteria and 'failures resulting from excesses in love'.

THE ICELANDIC PHALLOLOGICAL MUSEUM

Hé insbraut 3A, 640 Húsavik, Iceland
Telephone: (Iceland 00354) 561 6663 / 868 7966
www.phallus.is

'I have often been asked why I started collecting these things and I haven't any good answers. Somebody had to do it (!) and I wasn't interested in collecting stamps … I like to be provocative and maybe a wee bit eccentric.'

Sigurdur Hjartarson, curator

If a thing is worth doing, it is worth doing properly. On this principle, Sigurdur Hjartarson has made a point of collecting the 180 penises belonging to almost all the land and sea mammals that can be found in his native Iceland: including those of 50 whale species, a polar bear and 27 kinds of seal and walrus. If you wish to see and compare the phallus or the penis bone of the Arctic fox, the hamster, the black rat or the goat, then this is the museum for you.

The urbane Mr Hjartarson, a teacher and writer, started this collection in 1974. His attitude is a mixture of the scholarly and the tongue-in-cheek: 'Phallology is an ancient science which, until recent years, has received very little attention in Iceland, except as a borderline field of study in other academic disciplines such as history, art, psychology, literature and other artistic fields like music and ballet.'

Foreign animals are (partially) represented: skunks, polecats, raccoons, wallabies, even a bear and an elephant. Depending on the size of the organ and the provenance, the penises are displayed in special tanks or jam jars. There's a pair of earrings made from two penis bones of the stone marten, *Martes foina*.

And the best is yet to come: the museum has in its possession four legally certified gift tokens for future examples from Iceland's other native mammal, *Homo sapiens*. One of these, from the very generous Mr Páll Arason, is exhibited alongside the foreskin of a 40-year-old Icelander already preserved in formalin. Mr Arason has specified that the organ should be removed while his body is still warm, to improve its chances of perfect preservation. Mr Peter Christmann of Germany has submitted two photos alongside his gift voucher, while Mr John Dower of England and Mr Stan Underwood of America have provided plastic moulds in anticipation of their final donation. Mr Underwood's certificate shows that his wife, the current owner, also agrees to donate 'Elmo' on her husband's death.

A modest but immaculate whitewashed building hosts the collection, which is curated with care and detail inside the spotless pine-lined interior. The provenance of each specimen is listed. A sperm whale's phallus is described thus: 'An old male beached on the south coast in January 1992, hollowed, salted, dried, placed on a wooden plaque.' Another sperm whale, which died of intestinal blockage in 2000, contributed a penis that measures 170 centimetres (5'6"). Rather different in proportion to that of the house mouse, *Mus musculus*: 'Adult, penis and testicles, 2002, in formalin.'

Iceland's folklore is rich in monsters, and many images of these creatures are manifestly male. Among the museum's examples there's the masculine organ of the Njardvik Growler, *Homo/Monstrum terribilis Njardvicensis,* killed in Naddagil by Jón Bjórnsson, a farmer, in the middle of the 19th century. And that of the Beach-Murmurer, *Homo unipes, unimanus et luscus maritimus,* a one-legged, one-armed and one-eyed monster who tried to push people into the sea and murder them. There's also the penis bone of the enriching beach mouse, *Mus litoris loculpe-tatus,* reputed to draw money from the sea to swell the coffers of its owner. Not to mention the nub of the Nasty Ghost of Snael-fiall, *Umbra maleficia Snaelfiallenses,* a famous 17th-century ghost, guilty of many foul deeds in the western fjords.

The reader will be wondering about the museum gift shop. It does not disappoint: skipping ropes with phallus handles; a coat rack with specially carved pegs; lampshades made from dried bull scrotum; bow ties out of whale penis leather; and, of course, a nice line in photographic postcards unlike anything the folks back home are likely to receive from anywhere else.

NEWSTEAD ABBEY HISTORIC HOUSE
AND GARDENS

Newstead Abbey Park, Nottingham NG15 8NA, England
Telephone: (UK 0044) (0)1623 455900
www.newsteadabbey.org.uk

Newstead! what saddening change of scene is thine!
Thy yawning arch betokens slow decay;
The last and youngest of a noble line
Now holds thy mouldering turrets in his sway.

George Gordon, Lord Byron, from
'Elegy on Newstead Abbey', *Hours of Idleness*, 1807

Newstead Abbey suited George Gordon, Lord Byron, perfectly. It was a great Gothic ruin of a place, a true cradle for the cult of a Romantic hero-poet. The building, in fact, has a far longer pedigree than its most famous inhabitant, as it was originally constructed in about 1163 by Henry II as the Priory of St Mary. After Henry VIII suppressed the monasteries, Newstead Abbey was sold to the Byrons.

The celebrity poet was not the family's only black sheep. Byron's great-uncle William, the so-called 'Wicked Lord', murdered his neighbour and shot his own coachman. At an ornamental lake at Newstead he staged miniature naval battles. He shot 2,000 deer on the estate, stripped the ancestral parks for timber and sold off the contents of the house. All this from sheer depravity and a wish to bankrupt the estate for his son, who married against his wishes. But the son died first, clearing the succession for the man whom today's world knows as Lord Byron. It was said that on the day the 'Wicked Lord' died, all the cockroaches poured out of the house.

The young poet inherited Newstead in 1798 but with no fortune to attend to its dilapidations. It was leased out to a Lord Grey while Byron attended Harrow and Cambridge. It was some years before he began to take his friends there for what might now be called raves, fuelled by claret and attended by 'hand-maidens'. My Lord's preferred drinking glass was the skull of a monk mounted on a silver stem. It had been dug up in the former priory's burial ground. (Byron's own bedroom was haunted by a ghostly Black Friar.) Entertainments included fencing, indoor pistol-practice and teasing the wolf and bear that Byron kept tethered to the front door. From that front door he'd watched his mother's funeral cortege depart: he did not bother to join it.

Byron declared in 1809: 'Newstead and I stand or fall together ... no pressure, present or future, shall induce me to barter the last vestige of our inheritance.'

But he sold it to pay his debts in 1818, by which time he had moved on to partying in the Palazzo Mocenigo on the Grand Canal in Venice. His affair with his half-sister Augusta and a marriage dissolved amid rumours of brutal indecency had made him a pariah in Great Britain, where his homosexual dalliances could also have sent him to the gallows. Byron never returned.

Today the accommodation at Newstead is handsomely restored. The panelling gleams darkly. Luxurious draperies and rugs bestow on it a comfort that the hero-poet might have affected to despise. The Byron exhibits include some important manuscripts, portraits and also more personal possessions, including the shoe lasts that he was forced to wear in an attempt to correct his club foot. There's the ostentatious helmet designed by Byron for his ill-fated expedition to Greece in 1823. Byron posed in it for the dramatic portrait that helped define him as a Romantic icon. In the master bedroom, there's his canopied bed. Byron's study contains the poet's furniture, including a screen découpaged by his fencing master, Henry Angel.

There is also the brass collar of his dog, Boatswain, whose death is commemorated in one the poet's better pieces. Unlike some of his love poetry, this dirge does have the ring of sincerity.

Newstead's collections are not limited to Byron, though he is certainly the main draw for visitors. There are also architectural elevations showing the evolution of Newstead and relics from the medieval priory.

And for those of a romantic bent, the good news is that Newstead Abbey's Orangery is licensed for civil wedding ceremonies. No one need worry about the ghosts of the poet's own tortured marriage – Byron never actually took his bride to Newstead. She went to see it only after his death.

The Nitrate Ghost Towns

Santa Laura and Humberstone, Iquique, Chile

The peasant sells his cows,
his saddled horses
because they say in the north
you can earn fistfuls of money.
I'm going north, I'm going
to the nitrate-rich north
where I'll be a classy gentleman
with a cane.

A popular song among men
who worked the Chilean nitrate mines

A dark hulk of rusted metal broods on a lunar landscape. It's bigger than a beached battleship and weirdly beautiful. Flaps of loose corrugated iron clang as the wind hustles in from the arid pampas. Industrial architecture doesn't get more haunting than this. The hulk is Santa Laura, the wreck of Chile's great nitrate rush that started a hundred years ago. Nearby there's the company town of Humberstone, complete with school, theatre, hotel, church and stores, all echoing and empty in the hot, dry air. It literally never rains here.

The compelling thing about Santa Laura and Humberstone is the utter absence of Disneyfied prettiness. These are hard places, authentic down to the last floorboard and child's utilitarian desk, and yet there's also a wistful romance about it.

Once upon a time this place was crowded with workers from Chile, Peru and Bolivia, excavating nitrates from the hostile earth. Humberstone started life as a company headquarters or *oficina* known as La Palma. But a British magnate, James Humberstone, took over the operation, revolutionised the ore-refining technology, and turned the place into his private domain. By 1925 La Palma had been rechristened Humberstone.

Then, suddenly, the nitrate boom died. By 1960 the works and the town were abandoned to the encroaching sands, and time began to stand still at Santa Laura and Humberstone.

The whole town is a museum. The visitor wanders around at will, absorbing the atmosphere. The schoolrooms, with their rows of painted desks, are particularly evocative. The hotel dining room and bar still have their fading paint and a faintly festive atmosphere. At the back of the hotel, a surprise: an empty swimming pool, made from sections of a ship's iron hull. The theatre still has all its seats, but no audience. The marketplace has its little stalls, but no merchandise. In the company store a few items of old packaging are preserved, but what is mostly on display at this ghost town is emptiness.

At Santa Laura the main house is now a desultory kind of museum too – a tribute to the fact that you don't need audio-visual displays to recreate a powerful atmosphere. There are few signs, no explanations, but every breath you take inside the dusty building recalls the tough past. The rooms are starkly furnished. The windows are filled with views of the monolithic hulk and the desert. Threadbare dresses hang in crude wardrobes. Tired shoes are carefully paired on old trunks. Single iron beds are covered with thin quilts, the bravely vivid Depression colours gradually bleaching away to grey. Battered enamel kettles sit in glass cases, along with the packaging of everyday foods long ago consumed. Everything that you see has been abandoned by a real person who once used or wore it. The few visitors walk around the house in silence, for there's an overwhelming sense of intrusion into a private loss.

A mysterious sign hangs outside: 'Museum Entry Reaches Voluntary Thank You'. Somehow it makes sense – Santa Laura and Humberstone are what you make of them. With imagination, you can recreate the bustling town and noisy households for yourself.

There are other ghost towns in Chile but these two are the best preserved and quite easily accessible, just 45 kilometres (28 miles) inland from the port of Iquique. They were declared a UNESCO World Heritage Site in 2005.

THE EDEN KILLER WHALE MUSEUM

PO Box 304, Eden, NSW 2551, Australia
Telephone: (Australia 0061) (0)2 6496 2094
www.killerwhalemuseum.com.au

'[T]he whaling voyage was welcome; the great flood-gates of the wonder-world swung open, and in the wild conceits that swayed me to my purpose, two and two there floated into my inmost soul, endless processions of the whale, and, mid most of them all, one grand hooded phantom, like a snow hill in the air.'

Herman Melville, *Moby-Dick*, 1851

A most extraordinary relationship between man and beast unfolded in Twofold Bay, Australia, in the early years of the last century.

For season after season, a pack of killer whales, led by 'Old Tom', became the friends and colleagues of the bay's human whalers. For the killers and the fishermen had a common interest: catching baleen whales.

Old Tom's gang were identified by individual scars and markings. The local men gave them names – 'Hooky', 'Humpy' and 'Stranger'. Old Tom's pack would hunt down the baleen whales in open water and chase them into Twofold Bay. Then the bully boys would start 'flop-tailing' – churning up the water with their tails. Thus alerted, human whalers launched their boats.

It did not end there. Even after the whalers launched their harpoons, the killer whales would expedite each baleen's death by rolling over its blowhole to stop it breathing.

The only rewards that Old Tom and his friends accepted were

their favourite delicacies – the tongue and lips. After that they would swim away and leave the humans to take the remains of the baleens to shore.

Whaling continued in Twofold Bay until 1928, by which time it had ceased to be a profitable concern. Old Tom's body was found in Twofold Bay on 17 September 1930, and the discovery inspired the people of the town to create a permanent memorial both to the whale and their industry.

Visitors can now see Old Tom's skeleton at the Eden Killer Whale Museum, a clean, bright art-deco building perched on a hillside overlooking the Pacific Ocean. Even now, the museum provides a vantage point for viewing migrating whales, these days safe from both Old Tom and his human friends.

The museum is still managed by a small, enthusiastic voluntary committee. Exhibits include whaling boats, historical prints and portraits of key local figures. Old Tom is, of course, the starring attraction, and he's still a fearsome sight, with his 15-centimetre (6-inch) teeth and distinctive long beak gaping open right under the visitor's nose.

There's also the Bert Egan Memorial Lighthouse, a fully working replica containing original parts of dismantled historical lighthouses. Bert Egan was honorary curator at the Eden Museum from 1957 to 1982 and a fount of knowledge about the old whaling days.

Lecture programmes, walks and special exhibitions are offered by the museum, and the Davy Jones' Treasures shop sells merchandise, memorabilia and books to do with Twofold Bay's colourful past.

THE NEW ORLEANS HISTORIC
VOODOO MUSEUM

724 Dumaine Street, New Orleans, Louisiana 70116, USA
Telephone: (USA 001) 504 680 0128
www.voodoomuseum.com (somewhat out of date)
(For Voodoo consultations, contact John T. Martin
on 504 581 3824
or email at johntvoodoono@aol.com)

'This museum tells a unique part of New Orleans' culture.'
John T. Martin, Voodoo priest and curator

Hurricane Katrina dealt a tragic blow to the cultural life of New Orleans. Museums in the old French quarter weren't physically damaged, but, without visitors to support them, many couldn't afford to stay open.

Yet the mighty Katrina could not conquer the indomitable spirit of Marie Laveau (*c.* 1794–1881), the city's venerated Queen of Voodoo, an ancient religion that travelled from Africa to America in the slave ships. New Orleans vies with Miami as America's hotbed of Voodoo. Up to 10 per cent of New Orleanians still practise it. And even post-Katrina, the New Orleans Historic Voodoo Museum remains open not just for visitors but for Voodoo rituals and consultations.

The museum was founded in 1972 by Charles M. Gandolfo, whose own family escaped the slave uprisings in Haiti, hidden in barrels by a Voodoo friend and put on a ship to New Orleans. Mr Gandolfo, an artist, once ran a hairstyling salon. In this, he followed in the footsteps of the great Marie Laveau.

Marie Laveau was a free woman, a quadroon, meaning that African, Indian, French and Spanish blood ran through her veins. Originally a hairdresser and nurse during the yellow fever epidemic, she was well placed to learn everything about everyone in the town. She eventually became the all-powerful figure in the New Orleans Voodoo community. By the 1830s she was styling herself the Popess of Voodoo. She attended Catholic mass each day, and then performed her Voodoo rituals behind St Louis' Cathedral, with the church's full knowledge. She and her common-law second husband practised some remarkably successful fertility rituals: Marie bore fifteen children in eight years, including two pairs of twins and one set of triplets.

Charles Gandolfo passed away during Mardi Gras in 2001. His brother Jerry is now the actuary of the museum, while Voodoo priest John T. Martin presides over the spiritual aspects. He's assisted by Jolie Vert, an albino green python, and Hugene, a 5.5-metre (18-foot), 136-kilo (300-pound) Burmese python. The snakes represent Danballah, the serpent spirit who serves as a conduit to God. Mr Martin offers rituals, consultations and custom Gris Gris – bags containing protective charms. Mr Martin can be seen on the DVD of the film *Angel Heart*, which includes a feature on Voodoo in New Orleans.

An alligator's head and a broom greet the visitor, who passes through the gift shop to the History Hall, which tracks the slaves' odyssey to New Orleans, where they were forced to practise Catholicism. Then there's the Gris Gris room that explains the child-spirit Exu and various Ju-Jus – articles that drive away evil spirits. Also in this room are the blowfish and zombie whip which are used in the zombification process indigenous to Haitian

Voodoo. A zombie is an undead person whose soul has been traded to the devil. (According to Voodoo mythology, New Orleans piano-man Jelly Roll Morton was a zombie. His godmother traded his soul for hers after making a deal with the devil.) Finally, in the Altar room one can see an actual working altar as well as the wishing stump used and owned by Marie Laveau's daughter, who followed in her mother's footsteps.

The museum's store sells candles, incense and chicken-foot Ju-Jus, as well as Voodoo dolls. Contrary to popular belief, these dolls have a benign history. They were used for medical record-keeping. The practitioner would mark each person's doll with a history of their afflictions. Nowadays the passion doll is more popular – the user inserts some hair or nail parings from the object of desire into the doll's head and puts a pin in the body part that he or she wishes to inflame …

THE HASH, MARIHUANA & HEMP
MUSEUM

Oudezijds Achterburgwal 148,
1012 DV Amsterdam, the Netherlands
Telephone: (Netherlands 0031) (0)20 623 5961
www.hashmuseum.com

'Many woes will not be cured by all the herbs that grow;
Hemp has many bad and evil things put right and made them go.'
A German saying 'curated' by the Brothers Grimm

In the heart of Amsterdam's red-light district there's an inter-esting smell coming out of one of the buildings. It's kind of sweet and smoky. Relaxing, you know.

More than a million people have been drawn in since this museum first opened its doors in 1985. What they'll find inside is every manifestation of the versatile hemp plant and every pos-sible accessory for smoking it.

But hemp isn't just for fun. From earliest times, cannabis was associated with spirituality and meditation. Rastafarians still regard it as a holy plant. It has long been used as a medicine. Cannabis, as the museum's information boards explain, com-pares very favourably with legal drugs such as tobacco or alcohol when it comes to health side effects.

Although modern attention focuses on its hallucinogenic effects, hemp has a whole other life as one of the planet's most versatile, bio-efficient and respectable resources. Hemp was there when human civilisation climbed up the technological ladder. Without hemp, Gutenberg could not have printed the first Bible. Without hemp sails, Columbus would not have discovered America. What were the first banknotes made of? Even the Old Masters painted their works on hemp canvas. And without hemp sailcloth, Levi Strauss could not have made the world's first pair of jeans.

The exhibits chart the 10,000-year history of hashish and its production in Afghanistan and the Middle East, its consumption in the West, and its role in literary, jazz and pop cultures. Not to mention its special place in Amsterdam, where cosy cafés freely sell cannabis alongside their coffee and cakes.

Enthusiasts should make their way there in all haste, however, because even in liberal Amsterdam, the laws are now tightening and cannabis may yet become *flora non grata* – though it's unlikely that we shall see again the fervid persecution of hashish that took place in America in the 1930s, when posters described it as 'a powerful narcotic in which lurk *Murder! Insanity! Death!*' A film, *Reefer Madness*, was advertised with the catchline, 'Women Cry For It – Men Die For It!', and promised scenes of drug-crazed abandon.

The world of literature has always had its hash adherents. Charles Baudelaire co-founded the Paris Hashish Club. Friedrich Nietzsche declared: 'If one seeks relief from unbearable pressure one is in need of hashish.' Wilhelm Busch of *Max and Moritz* fame illustrated a cartoon epic about it. Fine art does not neglect hemp. The museum has a collection of paintings that show farmers harvesting it, ladies spinning it, sail-makers weaving it and, of course, friends enjoying it socially. Artists include David Teniers de Jongere, Piet Mondrian, Adriaen Brouwer, Adriaen van Ostade, Herman Saftleven and Hendrik Sorghe. There's a charming 'Jolly Hemp Primer' from 1942; an illustrated manual on how to grow the plant; a Japanese engraving showing a kimono decorated with hemp leaves; and a 'Medicina Antiqua' from the 9th century, when cannabis was considered an excellent cure for frostbite and sore nipples. Today it is known to ease the symptoms of glaucoma and eczema.

The heart of the exhibition is a grow room, where the actual plants can be viewed in hydroponic cultivation under special growing lamps.

The shop next door to the museum, Sensi Seeds, sells just what you'd expect. The museum's website links to Sensi Seeds' online store, where you can buy everything you need to grow, harvest, prepare and smoke cannabis. The museum has produced its own handsome coffee-table book, by Mathias Broeckers.

There's also an online forum on all matters to do with the plant. Plus you can research recipes for such treats as Chicken à la Marihuana ('Enjoy with your friends, just make sure you tell them what they are eating as they're sure going to know within 40 minutes'), Cannabis Crispy Treats and Hash Brownies as Mama probably never used to make 'em.

The Museum of Bad Art

580 High Street, Dedham Square, Massachusetts 02026, USA
Telephone: (USA 001) 781 444 6757
www.MuseumOfBadArt.org

'Artists who make it into the MOBA portraiture collection are oft visited by a unique, possibly extraterrestrial muse. Maybe one with rabies.' From the museum's website

This is the world's first (and at one time the only) museum dedicated to the collection, preservation, exhibition and celebration of genuinely and sincerely bad art.

The physical museum is located in the basement of a community cinema. The gallery displays 30 to 40 of the 400 pieces currently in the collection. Each work is presented alongside curatorial observations to help visitors fully appreciate the significance and meaning of the art – if any. The rest of the collection can be seen on the stylish website. MOBA has also published a glossy coffee-table book, *Museum of Bad Art: Art Too Bad to Be Ignored*.

The museum was founded in 1994 when curator Scott Wilson rescued the astonishingly awful painting now catalogued as '*Lucy in the Field With Flowers*, oil on canvas, by Unknown, acquired from trash in Boston'.

Today the museum's extensive holdings are divided into three categories: portraiture, landscapes and 'unseen forces'. Descriptions of the works are offered in traditional pedantic museum style, including the materials, size and provenance of the art, the latter being anything from 'church sale' to 'Salvation Army thrift store' or 'the artist's mother'. Most, however, have been sourced 'from the trash'.

'What makes a painting bad?' asks Wilson. He answers: 'I know it when I see it.' Passion is a key. Size is also important, he explains. The bigger the better. He also looks for garish colour and inappropriate frames. He draws the line at paintings on velvet. Those, he explains are bad taste. Bad art is better than that.

There's a conservation mission at MOBA, too. Wilson explains: 'Over the years, MOBA has received umpteen bequests from the Public Refuse System, a generous donor. As such, our first task upon accepting artwork into our collections is often dealing with safety issues such as pointy edges, broken glass and/or parasites.'

Highlights include *Peter the Kitty*, *The Circus of Despair*, *Two Trees in Love* and *The Haircut*, the last being a sculpture of found art featuring a barber's chair, scissors, dental floss and 'a fluffy white piece of the curator's cat'. This piece was specially commissioned by the museum, and one hopes the cat survived the donation.

Each exhibit is described in a witty parody of pretentious 'artspeak': the lurid *Mama and Babe* is acutely analysed: 'The flesh tones bring to mind the top-shelf liqueurs of a border bistro.' Of *Torment of the Soul*, the curator asks: 'What happened to his hand?' In *Sunday on the Pot with George*, he marvels at 'the almost careless disregard for the subject's feet'.

As at any self-respecting gallery, real and virtual visitors can also buy MOBA tote bags, mugs and posters featuring reproductions of exhibits from the museum. Fans of bad art can sign up on the website to receive the free MOBA newsletter by email.

There's another private collection of 'saved' art to be seen online at the Museum of Fred: www.museumoffred.com. The curator has collected art from thrift stores and classified it for display on his elegant site, which also provides an eloquent apologia for the social role of online museums.

THE INTERNATIONAL CARNIVAL AND MASK MUSEUM

10 rue Saint-Moustier, 7130 Binche, Belgium
Telephone: (Belgium 0032) (0)64 335741
www.museedumasque.be

'Almost everywhere, already in misty times, man has always con-
sidered it necessary to wear a mask in order to call on the gods or
the powers of nature, to confirm his own force and power, to assure
the cohesion of the community, to distract himself ...'

From the museum's website

Belgians, you may be surprised to read, are famous partiers, and none more so than the citizens of the medieval town of Binche, 50 kilometres (32 miles) south of Brussels. The Binche carnival has been staged continuously since the 14th century and was recognised as 'Immaterial Cultural Heritage' by UNESCO in 2003. The stock characters of the Binche carnival are Mam'zelles (men dressed as women), Pierrots, Arlequins, Paysans and above all, Gilles, of which more later.

Carnival season involves many rituals commencing weeks before Lent. During the 'Trouilles de nouille', the masked revellers make merry with unmasked people on the streets and in the pubs. It all comes to a climax on Shrove Tuesday, when even today up to a thousand men and boys of the town parade through Binche in an assortment of unique costumes. The Gilles start at dawn with clogs, shirts stuffed with straw and hung with bells, and masks painted with red moustaches and green spectacles. Waving bundles of sticks to ward off evil spirits, they march and dance to the beat of drums.

Later in the day, the Gilles swap their masks for airy hats crowned with ostrich plumes. Oranges are a big part of the fun – usually red-centred blood oranges – which are presented and thrown to the crowds with increasingly high spirits. The smell of split and crushed oranges perfumes the air. The party involves the whole town, and goes on into the early hours.

That's how they enjoy themselves in Binche. But masking and carnivalling are universal phenomena. In 1975, Binche opened its International Carnival and Mask Museum. The museum, housed in a former Augustinian monastery, has an international repertoire, displaying some 15,000 costumes and masks from all over the world.

Some masks are simple disguises. Others hide fears or long-ings, not just of the individual who wears them, but of a whole community. Some show humility in parleying with the gods. Others show larger-than-life confidence. Some parody human nature. More are simply meant to entertain – or terrify.

The museum's non-European collection (on the second floor) shows the ritual functions of the mask and the feast in relations between man and his gods. The visitor discovers the very different uses of masks within the cultures of the Indians of North America, the Africans, Asians and Melanesians.

In Europe, masking has been a constant element in folk cul-ture, a regular part of the festival calendar. The museum's first-floor exhibits show the diversity of ritual and iconography within Europe, ranging from southern Italy to the north of Russia. Naturally, there's a hall devoted to Binche's own amazing carnival, represented with both antique costumes and a special film.

The website, in French only at the time of writing, gives a good idea of the building and the collections. Guided tours of the museum, if booked in advance, are available in eight languages.

There's another carnival museum in Malmédy, near Liège, and two in Germany, at Kitzingen and Orsingen-Nenzingen.

THE MUSEUM OF MADNESS

Island of San Servolo, 30100 Venice, Italy
Telephone: (Italy 0039) 041 524 0119
www.sanservolo.provincia.venezia.it

Sto mondo xe na cheba de mati,
e i più sani sta de casa a San Servolo.
This world is a cage of lunatics,
and the most sane live on San Servolo.

Venetian proverb

A rriving on a summer's day at this picturesque green island, everything seems so cheerful. Students bustle in and out of the several university faculties on the island. Craftsmen beat out metal at a school that preserves dying artisan skills. There are various learned institutes, a café and an exceptionally beautiful church. But just a little research shows that this utopian place of spotless corridors, gardens and cloisters was not always quite so pleasant.

San Servolo became Venice's lunatic asylum at the beginning of the 19th century, and by the 1840s it housed many hundreds of patients. It was originally run by the kindly priests of the *Fatebenefratelli* ('doing-good brothers'), who were experts in pharmacy and surgery.

But San Servolo, isolated as it was, did not stay immune to the influence of fashionable French theories on the care of mentally ill people. The 'alienists' prescribed a strict seclusion from society. Treatments included forced cold showers and immersion in baths for up to twelve hours. Fearsome leather cuffs and buckles kept unruly arms and legs under control. The *camiciola di sostegno* or straitjacket soon came to be used on San Servolo, as were phrenological devices, used to diagnose personality defects through bumps on the head. Later there were electric shock therapy machines, lie-detector gloves and other well-intentioned but suspect medical technology.

One of the tragedies was that some of the patients were suffering not from psychological illnesses but pellagra, these days diagnosed as a vitamin B1 deficiency. A diet heavy on polenta and light on protein sent many poor people to San Servolo. Advanced pellagra manifests symptoms of mental disorientation and was therefore treated as madness, as were alcoholism and sexual excess. The good food and kind regime at San Servolo restored many to good health, but the stigma of a stay at the island must have been hard to escape. The asylum did not finally close until 1978.

The patients were originally housed in three wards: the Imbecilic, the Tranquil and the Dangerous. Each had its own exercise yard and refectory. Work therapy was considered very efficacious. A few noble madmen were taken in as paying 'guests', but most of the patients were working class. They were set to their original trades. At one time the asylum had a shoe workshop, an ironworks, a printworks and a carpentry studio. Music therapy was used in the later part of the 19th century.

In 1873 the women were sent to the neighbouring island of San Clemente (now a five-star hotel with swimming pool and conference centre, and for some years before that, the refuge run by Venice's cat charity, DINGO). The archives and equipment from both islands are now housed and expertly archived by the

IRSESC Foundation on San Servolo, where a fascinating museum opened to the public in May 2006.

You need to take the number 20 *vaporetto* from San Zaccaria. All visits are guided and must be booked in advance. The tour takes in the pharmacy with its beautiful majolica jars, the anatomy theatre and the museum itself, with its straitjackets, braces, buckles and, possibly most disturbing of all, its sepia photographs of patients' faces. From the 1870s, the island made a practice of recording the faces of the inmates on arrival, appending these to the scrupulous *cartelle cliniche* that itemised every detail of their lives, in such a prescriptive way that a diagnosis resulted.

There can be few more poignant documents to human misery than these admission photographs at San Servolo, sepia shots of faces staring blankly or in terror at the camera. 'After' photos sometimes show a marked improvement; other times mere blankness.

There's another museum dedicated to psychiatric treatment at Lund, Sweden. This displays artworks created by the inmates as well as equipment for testing, diagnosing, treating and restraining them.

And in Bern, Switzerland, there's the Museum of Psychiatry, also featuring artwork from the inmates among the equipment that tortured them. Most fascinating is the intricate, intense autobiographical work of the troubled Swiss artist Adolf Wölfli, who spent most of his adult life at Bern's Waldau Clinic, now the site of the museum. And in Lausanne you can see a collection of 'Art Brut', the work of lunatics, murderers and arsonists.

THE BOTTLE-PETER MUSEUM

Smedegade 22, Ærøskøbing, 5970 Ærø, Denmark
Telephone: (Denmark 0045) 6252 2950
www.arre.dk/uk/flaskepeter

'Keep this bottle well corked or the mermaids will get out!'

Peter Jacobsen

His real-life job was as a cook aboard steamers and sailing boats, but Peter Jacobsen's true obsession was making ships in bottles. He started when he was twenty years old. By the time he was 84 he'd made at least 1,700 of them and more than 50 big model ships.

Throughout his long life, he never varied his traditional methods and nor did he update his simple tools: a sharp pocket knife, a piece of wire, bamboo, wood, paint and putty. 'Bottle-Peter', as he came to be known, carved each ship out of wood, made the masts of bamboo, wove the rigging out of sewing thread, placed the putty inside the bottle and decorated the glass. Then he folded together the rigging, pushed the flattened boat inside the bottle, pulled the cotton threads and raised up the rigging.

In 1943, at the age of 69, Peter Jacobsen and his Scottish wife came to the charmingly somnolent and picturesque little island of Ærø, in southern Denmark. He made a bargain with the islanders: if they would give him the use of a house for life, then he would offer them a ready-made museum of 200 bottle ships and 50 big models. Other places in Denmark had refused, but Ærøskøbing said yes. It proved a wise move, for news of the unusual museum soon spread by word of mouth. By 1950 Bottle-Peter was receiving 35,000 visitors a year from all over the world, helping to make the little island a tourist magnet, with more visitors than the Danish National Museum in Copenhagen at that time.

The Second World War did not stop Bottle-Peter's production of ships: it proved an inspiration. He liked to make symbolic liberty bottles showing allied victories. One bottle showed a German ship being torpedoed. Of course, as he told visitors later, he had to wait until the war was over before he could put that particular bottle on display.

Bottle-Peter himself passed on in 1960, but his museum is preserved and his friends are still producing ships in bottles in the same way. One very unusual exhibit is Bottle-Peter's own headstone, which he crafted in his own inimitable way. It consists of a large cross inset with seven intricate ships in bottles: one ship for every sea that Peter Jacobsen sailed. He intended it for the churchyard where he's buried, but the local clergy had other ideas, so it remains his monument in the museum itself.

The craft of ships in bottles is thought to have originated in the 18th century, though the invention of clear glass in the 19th century allowed the craftsmen to perfect their art. Contrary to popular tradition, it was not always sailors who made the ships. Some of the most famous makers have been bank clerks or artists.

It has been suggested by one scholar that the ships were at one time a device to fool the excise men: that the little ships swam in bottles full of fine spirits.

While ships are the most famous form of miniature art inside bottles, many other scenes have been preserved in this way: crucifixions, bars, even scenes of gold-mining and smelting.

Given the popularity of the art form, there are many, many other museums of ships in bottles all over the world. One interesting difference: Japanese ships are usually shown sailing into the bottle, while Western ships sail towards the neck.

THE SALEM WITCH MUSEUM

19 1/2 Washington Square North, Salem,
Massachusetts 01970, USA
Telephone: (USA 001) 978 744 1692
www.salemwitchmuseum.com

'She afflicts me! She comes to me at night and torments me! She's a witch!'

Accusations made against the victims
of the Salem witch-hunts

In a welter of lies, fear and ignorance, nineteen innocent people were hanged in Salem, Massachusetts in 1692. They were condemned to death by hysterical schoolgirls and fanatical judges.

The museum that commemorates their story is aptly located in an atmospheric Gothic Revival building. Every half-hour the museum stages its narrated presentation of the tale, which has been designed, written and costumed by historical experts, and is based on actual trial documents. The visitor travels back in time through thirteen stage sets, reliving the savage spiral of terror and manipulation that led to the Salem witch-hunts, one of the most haunting and tragic episodes in American history.

The drama began in January 1692 when two children in the village of Salem fell ill and the local doctor diagnosed bewitchment. A group of young girls became 'afflicted' with hysterical symptoms. They accused their neighbours of making pacts with the devil in order to torment them with mysterious pains. Tituba, a slave from Barbados, was said to have coached the girls in devil lore. By summer, more than 150 people from around

Salem had been named by the girls and imprisoned, all defence-less against accusations of witchcraft and vulnerable to a law that did not require any more evidence than the ranting of a school-girl to send a person to the gallows: consorting with the devil was at that time a legal felony punishable by hanging.

The first victim, Bridget Bishop, was tried on 2 June and hanged on 10 June. She was followed by thirteen women and five men. In addition, one man was crushed to death in a particu-larly cruel form of execution. Seventeen others died in prison before the court was disbanded. Sense suddenly prevailed. A new court released those awaiting trial and pardoned those awaiting execution.

The Salem witch-hunts have always fascinated social histo-rians, psychologists and writers. Parallels have been drawn between the mass hysteria and betrayal of 1692 and the McCarthy anti-communist purges in America two-and-a-half centuries later. One interesting theory has emerged from research into the tragedy: it's possible that the 'afflicted' girls may have eaten rye bread contaminated with a fungal form of LSD.

A separate exhibition, 'Witches: Evolving Perceptions', traces the history of witchcraft, from the good times of the respected pagan wise women to the deadly witch-hunts of the 17th century.

The shop is stocked with a mixture of witchy apparel like cloaks and branded baseball caps, alongside tote bags, fridge magnets and serious history books. The catchphrase on the shop's merchandise is 'Stop by for a Spell'.

A good time to visit Salem is Hallowe'en, when the town stages a three-week-long Haunted Happenings festival. The

Salem Witch Museum is only one of a number of other-worldly attractions in the town: the Witch Dungeon Museum, Salem Witch Village, Salem Wax Museum of Witches and Seafarers, the Witch History Museum, the Witch House, the Pirate Museum and Frankenstein's Laboratory.

THE MUSEUM OF BURNT FOOD

Online at www.burntfoodmuseum.com

'I had a smokin' good time at the Museum of Burnt Food!'
Homepage testimonial

This wry anti-foodie website shows how food must suffer for its art. It celebrates notable culinary disasters with photographs and captions. According to its curator, Deborah Henson-Conant, the online food *noir* museum was founded in the late 1980s, when she left a small pot of Hot Apple Cider to heat, but was distracted by a long and extremely fascinating telephone call. By the time she returned to the kitchen, the cider had burnt to a solid cinder. This charred lump became the museum's first exhibit: 'Free Standing Hot Apple Cider'.

It was soon joined by 'Thrice Baked Potato', a study in what happens to certain foods that mingle so well with the oven environment that people sometimes forget to extract them, and 'Why Sure, You Can Bake Quiche in the Microwave', one of the more colourful exhibits. The 'Study in Pizza Toast' symbolises the curator's love-life blazing to a close: 'a moving reminder of how profoundly any culinary endeavour reveals the true inner desires of the chef. Note how the melancholy carbonised cheese recalls the empty ghost of a passionless union.'

There's a similarly sad message emblazoned on 'BUT IS HE JEWISH?', a blackened bagel, gift of the Benveniste Carbon Dating Service: 'This beautifully preserved specimen tells it all: a beloved food, object of gustatory desire, placed in the oven with the best of intentions – and yet, as so often happens, preoccupation with life's ephemera leaves the beloved alone, neglected, ultimately its heart (and in this case everything else as well) turned hard as stone.'

'King Tut's Tomato' shows the destiny of a fresh vegetable that spontaneously undergoes a process similar to mummification.

Like many virtual museums, this one 'brazenly' makes great claims for itself: that it contains more than 49,000 scorched, singed, seared and charred items, including no fewer than 2,000 specimens in the Hall of Burnt Toast; that it is visited annually by more than 25,000 people; that the research staff includes 45 post-nutrition food scholars and an extensive support staff. The exhibit wings and restaurant pavilion allegedly employ 27 full-time educators and food service workers.

However, the reader should take note: all this information is to be found on a linked site, www.improbable.com. What's more, the curator's life is not in fact spent entirely in the kitchen … when she's not concocting mistaken treasures, Deborah Henson-Conant writes orchestrations, songs and stories and plays electric harp as the soloist with symphony orchestras.

Happy cooking, and don't forget the museum's motto: 'To cook the museum way – always leave the flame on low … and then take a long nap.'

THE GORDON BOSWELL ROMANY MUSEUM

Clay Lake, Spalding, Lincolnshire PE12 6BL, England
Telephone: (UK 0044) (0)1775 710599
www.boswell-romany-museum.com

What do I care for a goose-feather bed,
With blankets drawn so comely, O?
Tonight I'll lie in a wide open field,
In the arms of my raggle-taggle gypsy, O.

Traditional Romany ballad

There's a touch of showbusiness magic to every Gypsy. Romany ancestry has been claimed by Jane Russell, Marlon Brando and Charlie Chaplin. And David Essex.

Perhaps that's because the Romany race have always been travelling entertainers. Some were bear-trainers, some acrobats, others dancers or singers. Gordon Boswell is a singing kind of Gypsy, and the star of two CDs – *The Romany Rye*, containing such songs as 'Raggle Taggle Gypsies' and 'Hot Asphalt', and more recently *Romany Yog, Songs for Stick-Fires Old and New*. Some of the tracks: 'The Thirty-Foot Trailer', 'The Wagon in Which I was Born', and 'The Poacher's Fate'.

When he's not singing, Mr Boswell (who's been filmed for the Discovery and History Channels) runs a unique museum of Gypsy history, which includes what's probably the world's largest collection of Romany photographs and sketches going back 150 years.

'I made this museum for my ancestors', he explains. 'They are dead and gone and I don't want them to be forgotten.'

Was it hard for a man with travelling in his blood to settle down and run a museum? 'No', says Mr Boswell, 'I have the best of both worlds. I preserve the memories of the past, I get to use the wagons and I live in a comfortable house.'

The Romany Museum is colourful in every sense of the word. The visitor first views fifteen vividly painted Romany wagons, including one of the oldest 'vardos' in existence today, also a fortune-teller's tent with cooking utensils, Gypsy saddles, boots and clothes. The brilliant Gypsy colours, Mr Boswell explains, are the palette of northern India, from where the Romany people migrated in the 1500s. Mr Boswell's own family were among that group, and his great-great-grandfather, Wester Boswell, helped compile the very first English dictionary of Gypsy dialect in 1860. The first wagon in the collection was built and lived in by Mr Boswell's father. It's a 'bow-top', wired like a hoop skirt.

Mr Boswell himself delivers an illustrated talk on the Gypsy ways of life and death, and the vardo-journeys made by himself and his wife ('Not Romany, but after 40 years of marriage, she's come 95 per cent our way.'). Finally, there's a visit to the stables to see the horses that pull the wagons, and a chance to browse the gift shop, where you can, of course, buy *Romany Rye* and *Romany Yog*.

That's the classic Romany Museum experience. But there's another way of enjoying its facilities too – on the road. George Boswell offers a special museum day trip for private parties – a seven-mile drive in the Romany vardo to a scenic spot, where there'll be a stick-fire and a traditional Romany steak cooked for lunch. With a bit of luck, there'll be singing around the campfire.

Mr Boswell does weddings too, in his luxurious glass coach. And also funerals – in his collection he has a sombre horse-drawn hearse 'to accompany solemn and dignified funerals' for when – another song from his repertoire – 'Hard Times Come Again No More'.

FREDERICK'S OF HOLLYWOOD
LINGERIE MUSEUM

6751 Hollywood Boulevard, Los Angeles,
California 90028, USA
Telephone: (USA 001) 323 447 3227

'Brevity is the soul of lingerie.'   Dorothy Parker

Frederick Mellinger believed that beautiful lingerie made women feel beautiful.

He started in New York with a small mail-order company. Soon Hollywood and its shapely stars lured him west. It was the making of him. Once women realised what he could do for them, they flocked to his studio. He provided foundation garments for some of the most famous breasts in the business, including those of Mae West and Marilyn Monroe. He was the first to sell 'scandalous' black lingerie (1946). He's also credited with the invention of the push-up bra (1948) and the thong panty (1981).

The first Frederick's of Hollywood opened inside an appropriately eye-catching pink-and-grey art-deco building on Hollywood Boulevard. The flagship store has now moved a little way down the same iconic street. Just a few steps from the Kodak Theatre (where the Academy Awards are staged), the new store's a paean to Hollywood glamour, with its Swarovsky crystal sconces and Frederick's signature colour scheme of red, gold and leopard. Women shopping here can even claim that their bra-browsing is educational, for among the current fashions there are changing capsule displays of great moments in underwear history.

In 1986 the original shop opened the world's first brassiere museum: Frederick's Celebrity Lingerie Hall of Fame. Over the years, Frederick's acquired or borrowed such illustrious underwear as the bra worn by Tony Curtis for his cross-dressing role in *Some Like it Hot* and the girdle that kept Ethel Merman in shape for *There's No Business Like Show Business*. Visitors have been treated to Phyllis Diller's training bra (labelled 'This Side Up') and the black-and-gold bustier worn by Madonna during her 'Who's That Girl' tour. Also, the fur-trimmed bra and negligee once worn by Cybill Shepherd in *Moonlighting*. There was even a pair of boxer shorts that protected the modesty of Tom Hanks in *Forrest Gump*.

The old flagship store was looted during the Los Angeles riots of 1992. Some items of delicate Hollywood lingerabilia disappeared forever. A period of financial difficulty ensued. But the company has relaunched with typical pizzazz, and the museum is still bravely restocking itself with new celebrity models. Each year Frederick's invites the owners of some of Hollywood's most famous bosoms to design an item of lingerie for a charity auction: pieces include such works of art as Sharon Stone's Butterfly Bra and Halle Berry's Animal Print Corset.

Frederick's plans to remount the original Hall of Fame in the near future. In the meantime this is a store with museum pieces, as opposed to a museum with a store.

Frederick Mellinger retired in 1984 and died in 1990, but his company continues to blaze trails in technology. In 1998, the company launched an H2O bra padded with water, and in 2003, the new engineering triumph was the Hollywood Extreme Cleavage Bra.

ANGRY JOHNNY'S KILLVILLE HISTORICAL MUSEUM OF THE STRANGE

Online at www.getangry.com

'So you've wandered off the beaten path and found your way to Killville? ... Eternal damnation is just a trigger pull away.'

From the museum's website

I t's said that when a native Nonotuck American comes across a Berkshire Mountain Monkey, he knows to lay down his spear, get on his knees and start to sing his death-song. For that fearsome creature is impossible to kill, and has been known to live for more than a day after its head has been severed.

The Berkshire Mountain Monkey is but one of the exhibits in this virtual museum, where the 'remains' of extraordinary animals are curated in scary photographs under which the visitor can read even scarier captions.

The homepage welcomes you to Killville, 'the Creepiest Little Town in New England', home of the eponymous Angry Johnny and the Killbillies – that's Angry Johnny himself on vocals, Goatis T. Ovenrude on banjo, Sal Vega on drums and Jimmy Rat Fink on bass. The site's really the band's – devoted to their own myth and their lyrics. These are best listened to in a speeding car, while 'song by song the body count continues to rise, and the broken hearts and busted dreams keep pilin' up on the ground'. Song themes include hard drinking, hard driving, death ('Hey Mr Undertaker …') and road-kill ('Poor Little Raccoon').

It's a clever concept: a whole – but far from wholesome – virtual hometown somewhere in western Massachusetts. And what a piece of American Gothic it is. Killville's a flood-ridden ghost town whose sins are just too filthy to wash away. It's the home of 'Stinky', the Killville Pond Monster, and the sinister Killville Crop Circles. Killvillians worship at the Holy Church of the Tree Rat, whose most fervent disciples eat broken glass, drink gasoline and swing rabid possums. But if you really want to get to understand the place, you need to take Ichibod Dudley's Killville Murder Trolley Tour of Death and Misunderstandings.

As you're speeding gratefully out of town, be careful not to run over the Western Massachusetts Flat Toad. No live specimen has ever been found, and all existing ones have been scraped off the road near Killville. Some day that puzzle may be solved.

In the meantime, the toad brings us back to the museum and its creatures, any one of which even a vegetarian would be only too grateful to see under his car wheel as opposed to coming at him in the dark.

There's the Northern Appalachian Pig Worm, whose bite has been compared to an alligator; the Taconic Chicken Lizard; the Two-headed Turkey; and Toady the Human/Frog, who appears in a sinister blurred photo.

Mummifying and pickling are the only things that could stop the local boys from going bad. So some of Killville's past citizenry is also on display at the museum. The museum proudly presents the One-and-a-Half-Headed Boy, the Pigfoot Boy and the Killville Giant, all dreadfully deformed and terrifyingly back-lit for their website mugshots. More frightening still are the infamous O'Connor sisters, Carla, Candy, Kitty May and Cassandra. They were convicted of eating seven overweight children and sent to the electric chair in 1925. They were denied their last request for 'a plump little urchin, medium rare'.

This is a gem among virtual museums for its consistency and wit. There's a real sense of something out there. Waiting for you.

THE SPAM MUSEUM

1937 SPAM Boulevard, Austin, Minnesota 55912, USA
Telephone: (USA 001) 800 588 7726
www.spam.com

'Just as every Elvis fan longs to visit Graceland, SPAM fans world-wide now have their own pilgrimage to make.'

From the museum's website

Like everything else about the cult luncheon meat, the SPAM Museum in Minnesota is larger than life, and just a little bit tongue-in-cheek.

For a start, the SPAM Museum is vast: 1,535 square metres (16,500 square feet) of interactive and educational games, exhibits and video presentations – a fitting tribute to the pop culture icon and American institution.

Visitors entering the museum lobby must pass beneath a towering wall of 3,390 cans of SPAM. A 122-metre-long (400-foot) conveyor belt runs through the museum, carrying more than 800 cans of SPAM. Visitors may don hard hats and smocks to take their places at a simulated SPAM production line, 'just like the folks who work in the real SPAM plant'. Or they can submit themselves to the SPAM Exam, an interactive quiz show.

The Global SPAM section features a world map showcasing the countries where SPAM is a staple and even a delicacy. A 1.5-metre (5-foot) model of a SPAMBURGER hamburger dangles above the exit corridor, adjacent to a huge burger-flipping spatula. Naturally, you can also watch Monty Python's classic SPAM skit, highlighting the ubiquity of SPAM in British greasy spoons.

Where did it all start? SPAM was born in 1937 in the factory of Hormel Foods, out of a marriage of 100 per cent pure pork and ham. The museum shows models of founder George Hormel at his desk with his son Jay. The new product was originally called HORMEL Spiced Ham, but the company held a contest to invent a catchier name. The winner, Keith Daigneau, received a prize of $100, a vast sum in those days, and typical of the mythical proportions of everything to do with SPAM.

SPAM had its own mascot, SPAMMY the pig, who also spawned a cult. In 1940 SPAMMY made a guest appearance on the George Burns and Gracie Allen hit radio show. During the Second World War, SPAM became a staple food for American soldiers serving all over the world – the museum proudly displays a letter from President Dwight D. Eisenhower about the important role SPAM played in feeding the Allied forces.

By the 1950s SPAM was taking over the world, with SPAM agencies established in Ireland, Canada, England and Venezuela. And 1959 saw the production of the billionth can of SPAM. Hormel upgraded its technology in the 60s, with the introduction of the hydrostatic cooker, which could turn out 350 cans of SPAM per minute. Not surprisingly, the 2-billionth can of SPAM hit the production line in 1970 and the 3 billionth just ten years later. The current total is over 6 billion. Smoked SPAM was introduced in 1971 and SPAM Lite in 1992. In 1998 SPAM rebranded its image: it now has a gold can and a label illustration of the SPAMBURGER hamburger. At the same time SPAM leapt onto the information superhighway with the launch of www.spam.com. These days, 122 million cans of SPAM are sold worldwide each year, with a can of SPAM purchased every three seconds in America.

On the website, you can join the Official SPAM Fan Club or shop in the SPAM gift catalogue – think sandals, earrings, candles, mouse mats, ice-scrapers, glow-in-the-dark scrunchies and lip balm, the latter being bubble-gum rather than SPAM-flavoured.

THE SHERLOCK HOLMES MUSEUMS

Conan Doyle Place, Meiringen, CH-3860, Switzerland
Telephone: (Switzerland 0041) (0)33 971 4141
www.sherlockholmes.ch

and

221b Baker Street, London NW1 6XE, England
Telephone: (UK 0044) (0)207 935 8866
www.sherlock-holmes.co.uk

'My name is Sherlock Holmes. It is my business to know what other people don't know.'

Sir Arthur Conan Doyle,
The Adventure of the Blue Carbuncle, 1892

Sherlock Holmes fell to a watery death at the Reichenbach Falls in Switzerland, after losing his final struggle with the evil Professor Moriarty.

The nearby town of Meiringen has honoured the British sleuth with his own museum, built in the undercroft of the former English church in the gardens of the Hôtel du Sauvage – the Englischer Hof of Conan Doyle's tale. This is the place where Sherlock Holmes spent his last night.

The visitor descends a winding staircase to discover a meticulous reconstruction of 221b Baker Street, the detective's fictional London home. The architects researched original builders' handbooks and contemporary building regulations to come up with their design, as well as tracking architectural clues in descriptions in the books.

The Sherlock Holmes societies of the world make pilgrimages to Meiringen on a regular basis, often in full Victorian dress. Lamentation Suppers are held. Wreaths are laid.

On the Holmes trail in Switzerland, fans should not miss the Sherlock Holmes Museum in Lucens, this one created by Sir Arthur Conan Doyle's son, Adrian, and featuring many personal possessions of the writer. Exhibits include a viper in aspic, personal correspondence and first editions. The museum's cat is known as Watson.

There's another Sherlock Holmes Museum in Baker Street, London. It's the first of its kind in the world to be entirely devoted to a fictional character, according to its curators.

Sherlock Holmes and Doctor Watson 'lived' at 221b Baker Street between 1881 and 1904. And they might still feel quite at home there today, so faithful is the recreation of the beloved refuge described by Arthur Conan Doyle.

The visitor climbs seventeen steps to the famous first-floor study and bedroom, where all the essential Holmesian accessories are in place: his papers, case notes, deerstalker hat, violin, Persian slippers, magnifying glass and chemistry set. Visitors may pose in the detective's famous fireside armchair, though they may not smoke his personal calabash pipe.

On the second floor is the bedroom of Holmes' ever-astounded assistant Doctor Watson. His quarters overlook the rear courtyard of the house. The museum exhibits Doctor Watson's diary, in which he wrote his personal notes on the case of *The Hound of the Baskervilles*. The landlady, Mrs Hudson, occupied a room at the front. Her current-day incarnation, in period dress, is available to answer questions.

The third floor contains wax models of scenes from the

famous stories. Professor Moriarty is shown in all his evil.

The museum's gift shop stocks Holmesabilia (including a deerstalker hat, a calabash pipe and a police whistle) and a large selection of books and DVDs. The museum boasts London's only working hansom cab.

MARVIN'S MARVELLOUS MECHANICAL MUSEUM

31005 Orchard Lake Road, Farmington Hills,
Michigan 48334, USA
Telephone: (USA 001) 248 626 5020
www.marvin3m.com

*'A sensory overload! Everywhere I look – sights, sounds! Curious!
The cacophony of noise has a tendency to blend together while
magically allowing you to zone in on one game or another simply
by standing in front of it …'*

David Landau, on Marvin's

B ring plenty of quarters. This place is the Shrine of Coin-Op,
the Holy Place of Pinball, the Altar of Neon, the Temple of
Gypsy Fortune-Telling.

Marvin Yakoda has crammed every inch of his 511-square-
metre (5,500-square-foot) museum with animatronic dummies,
model aeroplanes, video games, pinball machines, posters, neon
signage and children's rides. He started collecting his vintage
coin-ops in the 1950s and opened the museum in 1990. He's still
constantly adding to the collection, shoehorning in yet more
examples of wondrously garish popular entertainment.

It's the coin-opabilia that marks Marvin's out as a prince
among mechanical museums. For 25 cents you can operate the
'Bimbo Box' – no, not a lovely, empty-headed blonde, but a
mechanical orchestra of Polynesian monkeys who play a tinkling
tune. The same price buys you a look at the ghastly two-headed

baby, or a chance to test your courage on the 'Nerve-O-Meter': how long can *you* hold down that red button under the foaming jaws of the rabid dog? You can also test your love skills on two different machines, play a mechanical banjo, learn to fly a virtual helicopter and set in motion a horrid guillotining.

Then on to 'Harvest Time' – a scene of everyday farming life, charming until you learn from its hand-lettered display card that this coin-op was carved by the Butcher of Alcatraz, a murderer who killed an entire family of farmers in Iowa. After creating this model, the Butcher apparently attempted an escape from prison and then drowned.

Drop another coin in the slot, and there's the Spanish Inquisition with a selection of visceral tortures jerkily enacted in front of your eyes. Or behold the 'Drunkard's Dream', made in 1935 to show just what a tippler of that epoch might expect to see 'after one too many'.

There's advice on hand … In 'Ask the Brain', a lugubrious bald genius responds to your questions with mystifying replies.

Marvin's is a noisy place. It's not just the shouts and laughter of the visitors but the clacking, ticking, ringing and playing of all those vintage entertainment and pinball machines, the whirring of vintage fans, the barking of mechanical dogs and the smoke-snorting mounted buffalo head. One wonders about the electricity bill at Marvin's.

Children can take a ride in a rocket ship, on the 'Teeter-Totter', or on a carousel complete with gemstone-encrusted horses. Overhead there's a clattering fly-past of 40 antique model planes.

There's a replica of the electric chair from the infamous Sing-

Sing prison where over 30 people were executed between 1921 and 1950. A naked pin-up poster of Burt Reynolds has a hinged wooden fig leaf covering his modesty. But if the curious visitor lifts the tempting leaf, flash bulbs pop in a large camera hidden above.

Another display is P. T. Barnum's ten-foot Cardiff Giant. This is based on the tale of a monster faked up by one George Hull, a cigar manufacturer and atheist, after an argument with a fundamentalist minister. He made and artificially aged the giant figure. Then he buried it on a friend's farm. When it was 'accidentally' dug up a year later, Christian fundamentalists embraced it as confirmation of Genesis 6:4, which speaks of giants buried in the earth. Meanwhile, Hull himself made a fortune touring the country with his monster and charging 50 cents a look. The great American showman P.T. Barnum was inspired by the hoax to make his own giant.

The visitor leaves Marvin's with his ears ringing, his eyes bulging and a busy night's dreaming ahead. But there's one consolation. The clock on the entrance archway runs backwards, so you'll be a couple of hours younger than you were when you arrived.

The European Asparagus Museum

Am Hofgraben 3, 86529 Schrobenhausen, Germany
Telephone: (Germany 0049) (0)8252 909 8534
www.schrobenhausen.de

'Asparagus inspires gentle thoughts.'   Charles Lamb

Asparagus has always had a vague whiff of sensual luxury about it. It's long been considered a costly aphrodisiac. As far back as 304 AD, Emperor Diocletian decreed a price limit. In the Middle Ages, asparagus was prized as a cure for ills ranging from jaundice to haemorrhoids. But by the 16th century the long tender spears were on every noble dining table, a food fashion item that has never lost its exclusive appeal.

Asparagus season, or *Spargelzeit*, is a major culinary event in Germany. Each spring sees the grand cull of thick white stalks beloved by the Germans, Dutch and French – the green asparagus sold in America and Great Britain is little known here. The white stalks do not go green because they are protected from the sun by covering them with earth. Apologists for white asparagus say that this process retains more of the delicate flavour.

Germany has asparagus tourism the way other countries have religious pilgrimages. There's the Lower Saxony Asparagus Route and the parallel Asparagus Cycling Trail, a 750-kilometre (470-mile) circuit that starts and finishes in Burgdorf. The town of Nienburg elects its own Asparagus Queen every year. There's an Asparagus Sunday festival in Lüchow, an Asparagus Express in Bruchhausen-Vilsen and the Asparagus Cup equestrian tournament in Kirchdorf.

And naturally there's an asparagus museum or two. Appropriately enough, the Bavarian edifice devoted to the asparagus is partly housed in the tower of a ducal mansion and surrounded by a little park. Founded in 1991, it is proud to be the first collection of its kind in Germany.

Outside the museum, three life-size steel horses draw a special asparagus plough. Inside, the ground floor is given to the botany, history and technique of asparagus-growing. The first floor is dedicated to *Spargelessen*, asparagus gastronomy – the art of preparation and the accessories for the elegant presentation of the finished dish. There are beautifully coloured asparagus dishes made to simulate a bundle of the vegetable itself and many examples of asparagus tongs, the most extraordinary of which must be the pair that belonged to the Russian ballerina Anna Pavlova. Crafted by Fabergé, they were made from silver plated with gold.

Asparagus has inspired not just chefs and gourmands but also artists: the second floor of this gallery houses an exhibition of the asparagus in art. Warhol and Manet both succumbed to the discreet charm of the asparagus. The earliest known painting of asparagus is from Pompeii, and dates back to 10 BC. As a symbol of prosperity, asparagus featured in the still-life tableaux of the 17th century.

True devotees of the asparagus can walk the museum's 6-kilometre (3.75-mile) Asparagus Trail and observe the growing and processing of the plant.

This is not the only asparagus museum in Germany. There's another in Schlunkendorf, south of Berlin. Enthusiasts can also make a pilgrimage to the Asparagus and Mushroom Museum in Horst-Melderslo in the Netherlands.

THE MILLION DOLLAR MUSEUM

27 Carlsbad Caverns Highway, White's City,
New Mexico 88268, USA
Telephone: (USA 001) 505 785 2291

'I seldom go into a natural history museum without feeling as if I were attending a funeral.'

John Burroughs

White's City in New Mexico actually belongs to the White family. That's the whole town, including two motels, the Velvet Garter Saloon, a caravan park and a gift shop. But the jewel in the family's crown is surely its Million Dollar Museum.

In 1927 a Mr Charlie White staked a claim to 141 hectares (320 acres) of New Mexico. Around the same time he purchased an entire museum of 25,000 curios. Having acquired the collecting bug, Charlie White kept acquiring. In the course of his lifetime he doubled the number of exhibits.

No one knows why he called it 'the Million Dollar Museum', not even his great-great-grandson, Trey White, who now looks after the place. 'I guess he thought it sounded neat.'

The museum's still open to the public to meander around, guided only by the eccentric and colourful signage, nearly all handwritten.

'No snuff!' the visitor is warned on entering. Young Mr White explains that tobacco stains used to be a problem in the old days.

'Gentlemen only!' cautions the Kinetoscopic peep show in the lobby, though ladies are apparently permitted to try the coin-op electric chair. The peep-show lovely, by the way, reveals very little but her bloomers. Mr White explains: 'She undresses down to what we'd consider fully clothed today.'

Visitors move past the mounted heads of moose and deer down to the lower floor, packed as tightly with unexpected treasure as Tutankhamen's tomb. The Million Dollar Museum ticks up its worth in vintage cars, branding-irons, cuckoo clocks, bear traps, antique typewriters, distorting mirrors, weapons, stalactites, wind-up victrolas, old carriages, antique dolls and 'a 17th-century bath tub of the type used by Napoleon'.

The most valuable collection in the Million Dollar Museum is of European doll's houses, billed as 'the largest of its kind in the free world'.

There's a Hall of License Plates and a 500-piece miniature ranch carved by 'the Whittlin' Cowboy'. He did not omit the tiniest detail, from coyotes perched on rocks to a cowboy in the outhouse. The western theme continues with 'the Horniest Room in New Mexico' – several dozen longhorn cattle horns mounted on the wall.

Natural curiosities include mammal tusks and the preserved remains of a two-headed turtle, a two-headed rattlesnake and an 'angel-faced devil fish'.

For the anthropologists there are the skulls of an ancient tribe simply called 'the basket-makers'. These are appropriately accessorised: each skull is placed in a different basket. There's one entire basket-maker, mummified. Other skeletons repose in glass cases.

From more modern times there are photos of 'the severed arm of John Ketchum', a train robber who was brought to justice and hanged in 1901.

And finally, the most famous and saddest exhibit of all. Poor little alien baby. Six thousand years old. Alone in his glass cradle; alone in this cruel humanoid world. The baby boy was once thought to be a member of an indigenous New Mexico pygmy tribe, possibly a junior basket-maker. But then came the excitement of the 50th anniversary of the Roswell extraterrestrial incident, and an overexcited Swedish journalist claimed that the Million Dollar Baby could be none other than the offspring of the Roswell ET.

Indeed, the baby's skin is almost transparent and its eyes do slant up in a rather alien way ... and as Trey White says: 'No one really knows where it came from.'

THE HOUSE OF TERROR

Andrássy út 60, 1062 Budapest, Hungary
Telephone: (Hungary 0036) (06)1 374 2600
www.terrorhaza.hu

'The past must be acknowledged.'

Attila József, from 'By the River Danube',
Contemporary Hungarians on Late Hungarians, 1936

When even the website spells out its homepage to the sound of rifle fire, you know you're visiting a chilling place. Enter the museum itself and you'll be enveloped in suggestive music specially composed by Ákos Kovács. It expresses everything you need to feel under your skin about the House of Terror – the only museum of its kind in the world, a monument to all those who were imprisoned and tortured in this very building under two successive brutal regimes.

Andrássy út 60 was constructed in 1880 as an elegant private mansion. But from the beginning of 1937, it was occupied by the ultra-right Arrow Cross Party, and renamed 'the House of Loyalty'. It was in its basement that prisoners were incarcerated when, in 1944, the Hungarian Nazis formed a puppet government. In rounding up and exterminating Hungarian Jews, the Arrow Cross proved to be Hitler's loyal henchmen. In just two months, 437,402 Jews were deported to extermination camps in the Third Reich.

After the German defeat, the Soviets moved into power in Budapest. They joined up the cellars of the block to form a labyrinth of prisons. The State Security Police occupied the building until 1956. For several decades, Andrássy út 60 resumed a peaceful life as an office block. In the 1970s the basement became a club for young communists: the same basement where hundreds, perhaps thousands of people were tortured, some to the point of death.

In 2002 the House of Terror opened its door to the public as a museum to commemorate those who suffered and died inside it. Top avant-garde architects have adapted it, creating, for example, a black entrance awning with the word 'Terror' etched out of it, so that even the sun comes through that grim filter. Inside, theatrical lighting, reconstructions and hi-tech audio-visual displays are mixed with remnants of the bad old days – a Soviet tank, one of the sinister black cars that carried away so many victims for interrogation, propaganda posters and surveillance equipment.

The second floor of the museum chronicles the activities of the Hungarian Nazis. Other rooms show how the Soviets systematically stamped out social freedom in Hungary. Fifteen hundred people were tried for plots against the state, including teenagers guilty of graffiti and peasants who failed to deliver the prescribed food quotas. Resistance members were tried in batches and buried in unmarked graves. Suspicion was sown between family members – Soviet children who requested the death penalty for their own 'saboteur' fathers were held up as models. It was all too easy to fall foul of the regime. You could find yourself at Andrássy út 60 if you missed the 'half an hour of the Free People Day', or failed to applaud a party speech for long enough.

The first floor explains the brutal repression of the Church in

Hungary – a country where 70 per cent of the population was Catholic. There's a room devoted to the 'justice' system of the Soviets, which 'redistributed' what was left of war-torn Hungary's wealth. Hundreds of thousands were resettled in forced labour conditions, while their possessions were confiscated and became the property of party members.

The Hall of Tears in the basement, starkly lit in red, commemorates the 25,000 people who died in Budapest's 1956 revolution. Down there too are the former coal cellars used for prisoners of the regimes. Pliers, lighted cigarettes, rubber truncheons and electricity were the torture instruments of choice.

Leading down to the basement is the staircase Gallery of Victimisers – those individuals who were responsible for crimes against humanity during the two regimes.

The exhibitions are labelled in Hungarian, but there's an English audio-guide and written information available. The online gift shop features a truly interesting array of merchandise – blank arrest warrants, candles in the shape of Stalin and Lenin, and a fridge magnet showing a pig with machine guns.

THE MUSEUM OF MENSTRUATION

Originally based in New Carrollton, Maryland, USA,
but now online at www.mum.org

'Get out the crime scene tape.'

A reader's favourite euphemism

This site is a serious and wonderfully comprehensive treatment of the history and culture of menstruation. The tone is sometimes light, sometimes indignant, but there's nothing superficial or sniggering about the MUM.

The curator, Harry Finley, presents a fascinating history of ignorance and enlightenment, every aspect of menstruation relentlessly cross-referenced and linked. This massive site contains not only photographs and explanations of Mr Finley's unrivalled collection of menstrual apparatus, but a wealth of literature and original advertising material, all scanned and presented online, such as *Marjorie May's Twelfth Birthday*, and a Kotex puberty and menstruation booklet from 1935 in which a mother explains the forthcoming physical changes, with abundant product placement.

From 1994 to 1998, Harry Finley ran the museum from his home. He has now posted it online instead. At the time of writing this book he was still looking for a permanent home for his 4,000 artefacts, including antique packaging, advertising, vaginal douches, tampons through the ages, a plastic sanitary apron and a dress made from menstrual cups.

Mr Finley came to the subject via his work as an art director with an interest in packaging design. He seems, from his own account and those of journalists who have interviewed him, a very sane person, with a talent for research, a generous spirit and a gentle message – that menstruation is not a vile disorder but a natural bodily function. He exposes cynical companies that have exploited feminine insecurities and debunks many menstrual myths and taboos.

'MUM's the word!' comments Mr Finley, 'MUM being the nickname for the museum, playing of course on the expression that means "Be silent" [about menstruation].'

Like most active and popular websites, MUM has its share of reader stories, personal accounts of menstrual catastrophes and triumphs.

These readers have also contributed an awesome list of euphemisms for menstruation, among which are to be found: 'Aunt Flo is visiting'; 'chocolate time'; 'the Communists have invaded the summer house'; 'the Venetians have arrived!'; 'I can't churn the butter today'; 'spending a week at the Bates Motel'; 'walking along the beach in soft focus' (a reference to television advertising of sanitary products); 'the sharks are circling' (although elsewhere on the site the learned Mr Finley cites an academic paper proving that sharks are not attracted to menstrual blood); 'get out the crime scene tape'; and 'George Clooney is visiting' (presumably a reference to the gore-laden hospital TV drama ER).

For tampons, the log references include 'Dracula's tea bags' and 'smoking a white owl', and for pads, 'mouse mattresses'.

THE PRESIDENTIAL PET MUSEUM

51 Maryland Avenue, Annapolis, Maryland 21401, USA
Telephone: (USA 001) 410 280 8850
www.presidentialpetmuseum.com

'Having pets humanises our presidents. We get a warmer feeling about them knowing that there is a pet in the White House.'

Claire McLean, curator

Woodrow Wilson had a ram that ate tobacco. Calvin Coolidge kept a virtual menagerie, including two leash-trained raccoons (named Rebecca and Horace), a bobcat called Smokey, a wallaby and a pygmy hippo. Theodore Roosevelt had a badger named Josiah and the Kennedys owned a rabbit called Zsa Zsa. Martha Washington kept a parrot. The White House has hosted at least 400 pets over the centuries, mostly dogs, horses and cats, but there have also been an elephant and even an alligator, the latter given to John Quincy Adams by the Marquis de Lafayette. Mrs Louisa Adams, meanwhile, kept silk-worms. These days most presidents help keep their image in soft focus with a photogenic dog or cat, whose celebrity status can at times outshine even their owner's.

The Presidential Pet Museum was founded in 1999 as a repository of information, artefacts and items related to the presidential pets. It all started in 1985, with a portrait of Lucky (President Reagan's Bouvier des Flandres) made from the dog's own fur. The curator of the museum, Claire McLean, a Bouvier expert, was invited to the White House for the privilege of grooming and clipping the Reagans' dog. Mrs McLean took the liberty of bringing some of Lucky's clippings home, and they were later fashioned into a portrait. The idea of a museum of presidential pet memorabilia was born.

Today the museum includes over 500 items of interest displayed 'for lovers of pets, presidents and pet trivia'. There's the cowbell from Pauline Wayne Taft, the last cow to graze the White House lawn, plus a wealth of photographs of presidents and their wives with their various pets. The visitor sees exhibits about Nelson, George Washington's horse; Lyndon B. Johnson picking up his beagle, Him, by the ears; and, of course, the Clinton family's famous Labrador Buddy and cat Socks. Naturally, the museum features all the latest White House pets, including Miss Beazley, a new addition to the family; Barney (there's a life-size bronze of this popular Scotch terrier); and Spot, a springer spaniel (recently deceased).

Some presidential pets had witty names: Amy Carter briefly owned a dog called Grits and a Siamese cat named Misty Malarky Ying Yang. Caroline Kennedy's pony went by the name of Macaroni. President Hoover owned a police dog called King Tut. Richard Nixon's Irish setter answered to Kim Timahoe. The bulldog of Calvin Coolidge was named Boston Beans and his canaries were called Nip and Tuck.

In the shop and online you can purchase Presidential Petibles, a collection of plush toys based on the original animals; also statuettes of cats and dogs, and models of Airforce One; talking action figures of Presidents Washington, Clinton and Lincoln (whose life was once saved by his dog Honey); and (hurry!) rare limited-edition President George W. Bush/Cheney inaugural Beanie bears.

THE BRITISH LAWNMOWER MUSEUM

106–114 Shakespeare Road, Southport,
Lancashire PR8 5AJ, England
Telephone: (UK 0044) (0)1704 501336
www.lawnmowerworld.co.uk

*'Don't let the grass grow under your feet! It's mower interesting!
Have even mower fun!'*

From the Lawnmower Museum brochure

The world's first lawnmower was the brainchild of Edwin Beard Budding. In 1830, the inventor was working at a wool mill in Stroud, Gloucestershire, where he designed a machine to trim the nap off cloth. His next innovation was to use the same contraption to cut grass. When people said he was mad, he took to testing the machine at night so no one could see him.

Budding had the last laugh. Not only did his invention catch on all over the world, but some of the greatest names in engineering have since been associated with the humble lawnmower, with models produced by Rolls-Royce, Royal Enfield and Hawker-Siddeley. These princes of the lawnmower industry are displayed at the British Lawnmower Museum, alongside 'celebrity' lawnmowers belonging to Princess Diana, Brian May, Prince Charles and assorted television personalities.

The museum, which now hosts over 400 exhibits, was created by ex-racing champion Brian Radam, whose family garden equipment business started in 1945. All the antique lawnmowers are restored to pristine condition and carefully explained, with much editorial comment from the expert curators.

The Lawnmower Museum is as much about social history as a deep pride in British engineering and ingenuity. An early hovercraft model, for example, is shown in its original blue colour, and the curators explain that it was only after Flymo surveyed 2,000 women that the trademark orange was chosen.

Naturally, Budding's first machine is there – it's unusual by today's standards in that it required two operators, one pulling, one pushing. There's a car designed by a lawnmower company, Atco, which was used for training people to drive during the Second World War. There's the popular 'Willing Worker', shown with its original advertising, and the Jerran & Pearson Water Cooled made in 1926. The Lawnmower Museum reckons that this is the best lawnmower ever made. Not surprisingly, it cost twice as much as a car in 1926.

The museum boasts the largest toy lawnmower collection in the world, as well as restored garden machinery and memorabilia from before the invention of the lawnmower. Its workshops restore rare antique models – the museum maintains a database of 600,000 spare parts for vintage lawnmowing machines. Meanwhile, its archives conserve many fascinating manuscripts including 500 original patents dating back to 1799. The collection of lawnmower manuals is a history of graphic design in itself.

And if you cannot make it to the museum itself, DVDs and videos of the collection are available by mail order. These feature catchy music written and performed by Doug Miles, a direct descendant of Edwin Budding. For a taster, go to the website and make sure you have the volume on. The website is well organised and lavishly illustrated, with links to lawnmower racing associations around the world.

The Museum of the Devoted Wives

Rathaus, Marktplatz, 7102 Weinsberg, Germany
Telephone: (Germany 0049) (0)7134 512139
www.weinsberg.de

'There is nothing in the world like the devotion of a married woman. It's a thing no married man knows anything about.'
Cecil Graham in Oscar Wilde's *Lady Windermere's Fan*, 1892

It's not often that devoted wives get a museum devoted to them, so this one definitely qualifies as unusual. It commemorates an irresistible story of not just wifely devotion but physical strength and lateral thinking.

In December 1140 the forces of the Holy Roman emperor surrounded the German town of Weinsberg. A rescuing army was soon demolished and hope faded. But the townspeople, led by the Duke of Welf, still refused to surrender, displaying a stubborn truculence that roused the ire of the new emperor, previously known as Duke Konrad of Swabia. He proclaimed his intention to teach them a lesson, by executing all the men inside the city walls and burning Weinsberg to the ground. The women, declared Konrad, would be allowed to leave, along with whatever personal possessions they could carry on their shoulders.

When the appointed time came for the wives to leave, the gates of the town were flung open to reveal an astonishing sight. First the Duchess of Welf tottered down the hill, carrying something large and heavy. She was followed by the rest of the townswomen, all buckling under their burdens. The surprise was this: the devoted wives of Weinsberg had put aside their silks and jewels, choosing to carry their husbands on their shoulders. The unmarried women carried their fathers or brothers. The men thus passed out of the town unharmed, and the women of Weinsberg earned the admiration of even the enemy soldiers (who were, perhaps, wondering if their own wives would have shown the same wit and devotion).

Konrad permitted the wives of Weinsberg to get away with their cleverness, saying: 'An emperor always keeps his word.'

The once-besieged castle above Weinsberg is today known as 'Burg Weibertreu', which translates roughly as 'the Castle of Female Fidelity'. It nestles on a rounded hill above rich vineyards to the north of Baden-Württemberg, in the district of Heilbronn. The nearby town's name is derived from the German word for vineyard, and indeed wine is the area's other claim to fame.

Weinsberg was severely damaged by Allied bombs during the Second World War. However, the devoted wives were not to be sent into obscurity – an airy and elegant new museum opened in the reconstructed town hall in 1987.

Not surprisingly, the story of the wives has proved an attractive subject for artists over the centuries. The museum hosts a collection of 60 works of art based on the tale, including engravings, sculptures and paintings not just from Germany but also from French and Dutch masters. Nicholas Giubal's 18th-century painting shows the healthy, buxom wives rushing around as if in some kind of village fair event. Frans Francken's 17th-century oil concentrates on the well-justified amazement of the soldiers as the ladies stream out of the castle gates.

While Weinsberg's women are probably the most famous, it must be said that there are similar legends about besieged and clever wives associated with many other castles and walled cities in Europe.

THE BREAD AND PUPPET MUSEUM

753 Heights Road, Glover, Vermont 05839, USA
Telephone: (USA 001) 802 525 3031 / 525 1271
www.breadandpuppet.org

*'Since this Museum replaces the traditional museum's ideal of
preservation with acceptance of more or less graceful and inevitable
deterioration, consider making your visit sooner rather than later.'*
Timely advice from the Bread and Puppet Theatre's brochure

A weathered dairy barn from 1863 holds a huge surprise.
Crossing the hand-hewn stone threshold, the visitor is con-
fronted by the huge papier-mâché faces of butchers, bishops,
beasts and soldiers. They are all characters retired from shows
staged by the quirky, thought-provoking Bread and Puppet
Theatre. The largest of the masks measures 5.5 metres (18 feet)
from chin to forehead.

Two floors of the giant barn host hundreds of these ghostly,
colourful creatures with their vivid expressions of greed, longing,
fear and love. Some pose in scenes from their original stories.
Others are grouped sociably as if gathered together of their own
accord for a satisfying gossip. They seem part of a gigantic,
eccentric family – not surprising, as these fantastic, fragile
creatures are all the conceptions of one man.

The story of the Bread and Puppet Theatre began in New
York's Lower East Side in 1963. The founder, Peter Schumann,
was a sculptor and choreographer. His very first theatre, on
Delancey Street, was called the Bread and Puppet Museum. Ten

years later he opened a second venue at Goddard College. This one went by the title 'Vermont's First Papier-Mâché Cathedral or The Art of Impermanence'. By 1975 the theatre had moved to Glover, in north Vermont, and taken over the old barn for its archive of puppets, banners, scenery and artwork. The company travels all over the world to perform its shows.

Ever since the early days, Schumann has designed all the masks in clay. The large-scale puppets are then constructed by a dedicated team of puppeteers, often using found materials such as packing cardboard, reject clothing from rummage sales and baling twine. The papier mâché is made from brown paper and corn starch paste.

The finished masks, according to the theatre company, are 'a prodigious mix of Romanesque, German Expressionism and Potato-Nose Naturalism'. Forty years of creativity have filled the barn to the brim, and inside there's a sense of gentle disintegration that reflects the principles of the Bread and Puppet Theatre, inspired, as its protagonists write, by 'the poverty of the poor, the arrogance of the war-mongers, the despair of the victims … And, naturally, all this will decay in due course.'

The theatre's productions are not limited to the stage. The puppets have also taken to the streets. During the Vietnam War, for example, the Bread and Puppet Theatre staged huge processions in New York, joined by hundreds of supporters. Productions still centre frequently on environmental and world-peace themes, and are muscled by local volunteers given just a few hours' rehearsal time. The company insists on spontaneity and forbids elitism, preferring to be true to its roots in traditional carnivals, perennial feasts and grass-roots protests. In recent years they have performed, for example, their *G-8 Oratorio* and an *Insurrection Mass with Funeral March for a Rotten Idea.*

This museum opens its doors from June until the end of October. It runs on a shoestring, manned by volunteers and funded by donations and sales of goods on the premises. Without any heating, the museum is usually snowbound in the winter months, and visitors prepared to brave the cold should phone ahead to make an appointment.

Finally, why Bread and Puppet Museum? At most performances the company distributes bread and aioli to its audiences. The bread is baked in an improvised brick oven on site by members of the team. The Bread and Puppet Theatre is available for bookings anywhere in the world – the players' only stipulation is that their hosts provide 400 bricks and an outdoor site near the performance space so that the bread may be freshly baked.

THE SMALL MUSEUM OF THE
SOULS IN PURGATORY

Chiesa del Sacro Cuore del Suffragio,
Lungo Tevere Prati 12, 00193 Rome, Italy
Telephone: (Italy 0039) 06 6880 6517

'My hands together clasp'd,
And upward stretching, on the fire I look'd,
And busy fancy conjur'd up the forms
Erewhile beheld alive consum'd in flames.'

Dante Alighieri, 'The Vision of Purgatory'
from the *Divine Comedy*, 14th century

After death, but before entering heaven, the soul must dwell in purgatory until it atones for its earthly sins. This religious precept, one would think, is wholly unprovable, as no one has ever come back from the grave to verify it.

But there are some scraps of tangible evidence, if you choose to believe them and can make your way to Rome to see them. In one small room in a neo-Gothic church, the visitor can view actual objects singed by the burning hands of souls in purgatory and photographs of other ghostly manifestations from the world beyond life.

It all starts to make sense when one understands that the soul's time in purgatory can, allegedly, be lessened by the fervent prayers of loved ones still dwelling on earth. And so, these hand-prints, which apparently appeared in bibles and breviaries and on nightcaps, were thought to be appeals from the dead for lustier prayers to speed them on their way to heaven.

The exhibits come from France, Belgium, Germany and, of course, Italy. The small collection began around a century ago, though some of the items are much older. The objects were hunted down by a French priest, Father Viktor Jouet, who was inspired by a miraculous vision he experienced during a fire inside the church in 1897. As the flames raged, the altar of Our Lady of the Rosary proved impervious, and an image appeared on the wall, burnt by the smoke, of a suffering face. Jouet was convinced that it showed a soul in purgatory, painfully expiating his sins. Thereafter it became Jouet's mission to collect as much literal evidence of purgatory as he could find on his travels around Europe. He also founded a magazine, *Purgatory*.

This is one of the tiniest museums in Rome, but it is also one of the strangest. The visitor walks down the right aisle of the relatively modern church of the Sacred Heart of Sufferance. Next to the sacristy there's the room that houses the display.

What's here? A nightcap with a hole apparently burnt there in 1875 by the soul of Luisa le Sénèchal, as a message to her husband to hurry along to mass and pray for her. There's a prayer book with three marks described as 'fingerprint burns' on the cover. These belonged to Palmira Rastelli, late of Rimini, nudging her brother to do his duty for her soul in 1870. There's a shirt from Giuseppe Leleux of Mons. This item carries the imprint of a burning finger that appeared there on 21 January 1789. Margherita Dammerle d'Erlingen left a scorch mark on her prayer book. Also exhibited is the coat of an Italian sentinel who, one night in 1932, was standing guard in front of the cenotaph of King Umberto I. The ghost of the assassinated Umberto placed a burning hand on the shoulder of this sentinel, charging him to deliver a message to Victor Emmanuel III.

Among earlier exhibits is an image of a burning handprint said to have been left on a nun's apron in 1696. The victim died of plague, but wanted another sister to do her best for her. There's also a wooden tabletop scorched with a purgatorial message.

Finally, there's a photo of the suffering face that appeared on the church wall – the original apparition that persuaded Father Jouet to commence his quest for other proofs. The visitor can decide whether Jouet's imagination was fevered – or inspired.

THE HOPALONG CASSIDY COWBOY MUSEUM

15231 SW Parallel Road, Benton, Wichita, Kansas 67017, USA
Telephone: (USA 001) 316 778 2121
www.prairierosechuckwagon.com/hopalong_cassidy_
museum_at_prair.htm

'I grew up in Nebraska, raising cattle and horses. We didn't go to many movies, but I remember when my father bought a television set. It was the first one I had seen. When the delivery man hooked it up and turned it on, the first thing that came on was Hopalong Cassidy. So it is a special thrill for me to be the curator for the Hopalong Cassidy Cowboy Museum.' Orin Friesen, curator

Orin Friesen is not alone. There was a time in the happy, innocent 1950s when you couldn't avoid Hopalong Cassidy, even if you wanted to. Turn on the television – there was William Boyd in the role of America's favourite cowboy hero. His face was printed on your milk cartons, on your lunchboxes, on your cookie jar. The toy shops were full of Hopalong dolls. There he was on the cover of *Life* magazine. Thousands waited in line for a glimpse when William Boyd made public appearances in cities and towns across the country and around the world.

Unlike Buffalo Bill Cody, Hopalong Cassidy was a fictional creation. The affable cowboy was dreamt up by the writer Clarence E. Mulford in 1907. William Boyd played the part in 66 movies, 52 TV episodes and 104 radio shows made over an incredible 30 years. By the time Hopalong's star had faded into the west, more than 2,500 items of Hoppy merchandise had been licensed. Teenage Mutant Ninja Turtles – eat grass!

William Boyd went to the dude ranch in the sky in 1972. Now we have the Terminator and other grim celluloid reapers, but there's a little place in Kansas where Hopalong's memory is forever kept warm. The Hopalong Cassidy Cowboy Museum is located on a working cattle ranch, 24 kilometres (15 miles) east of Wichita, Kansas, in Butler County. It contains 930 square metres (10,000 square feet) of exhibition space filled with stills, movie posters, costumes and personal items that once belonged to William Boyd. Visitors can view whole films and TV shows in the next-door Hopalong Cassidy Bar 20 Movie Theatre.

Other parts of the exhibition are devoted to equally famous Hollywood cowboys, including Roy Rogers, Gene Autry, Dale Evans, John Wayne and Tagg Oakley.

Hopalong Cassidy was undoubtedly king of the cowboy merchandisers. Hoppy was the first character whose image was legally 'licensed' for printing on school lunchboxes. It is the Hoppy merchandise that forms a large part of the collection and is cleverly displayed in room sets that illustrate the pervasiveness of Hoppy in American family life in the 1950s. There's a recreation of a young boy's bedroom from the period, complete with Hoppy toys, clothing and collectables. There's a Christmas tree with an entire range of Hoppy gifts beneath it, a kitchen with Hoppy lunchboxes, cookie jars and food.

Nostalgia buffs will be relieved to hear that a small collection of Hoppy merchandise is still available. It ranges from the simple Hopalong Cassidy Cowboy Museum Collector Thimble ($4.00) to the $250 Hopalong Cassidy Gold Edition Cookie Jar, which comes with a certificate of authenticity signed by Grace Bradely Boyd (Mrs Hopalong Cassidy). And just $25 will buy you a full-size 1.9-metre (6'3") Hoppy cardboard cut-out in full colour.

Speaking of food, few leave this museum hungry. The museum shares the ranch with the Prairie Rose Chuckwagon Supper. Visitors can also ride the Prairie Rose Express around the grounds until the supper bell rings promptly at 6.30pm.

THE FOOTWEAR MUSEUM

Avenida de Chapí, 03600 Elda, Alicante, Spain
Telephone: (Spain 0034) 965 383021
www.museocalzado.com

*'And what shall we say about shoes? What shall we say about the
great variety of prisons for our feet?'*

Azorín, pseudonym of Spanish writer José Martín Ruíz,
'fittingly' from Alicante

In English, we say 'like a kid with a new toy'. In Spain, they say
'como niño con zapatos nuevos' – like a kid with new shoes.

That gives some indication of the veneration in which
footwear is held in fashion-conscious Spanish culture. There are
several shoe museums in Spain, but the most glamorous is this
one in the province of Alicante.

This is a museum that takes shoes seriously. It organises
several awards, including one for the best shoe crafted in Spain
each year. The curators see the shoe as 'an expression of our idio-
syncrasy; as the fetishist's delight; as a marker of social class; as
the tip of the iceberg in the clothing revolution (!); as a friend of
comfort and ergonomics and enemy of tightness and corns'.

The Footwear Museum was established in 1992, initially to
preserve the traditional techniques, craftsmanship and tools of
the footwear industry, which has a strong history in this part of
Spain. Increased mechanisation meant that the age-old crafts
were at risk of being lost for ever. Out of this initial idea has
grown one of the largest collections of shoes – more than 15,000
pieces – and shoe-abilia in the world.

The museum has four rooms for permanent exhibitions, one for temporary exhibitions, a specialist library containing everything to do with the world of shoes, and a shop that sells miniature shoes as keyrings.

The Footwear with History section features shoes belonging to famous people from all walks of life: sports personalities like Seve Ballesteros, flamenco dancers such as Antonio Gades, and even the King and Queen of Spain. There's the pair that Pope John XXIII wore to his investiture, as well as the lasts (shoe forms) of Princess Diana and Queen Elizabeth II. The museum showcases the current winner of the Guinness World Record for the largest shoe – it's size 525. It also has a replica of the million-dollar diamond and platinum shoes worn by Laura Elena Harring for the 2000 Oscars.

The Footwear Design section shows styles created by famous designers such as Paco Rabanne, Salvatore Ferragamo and Charles Jourdan.

In another section, the museum interprets the whole history of humanity as told through footwear. There are displays of wooden shoes from different cultures – Egyptian sandals with wooden soles, Moorish *alcorques* made of wood, and Renaissance clogs with wooden soles 20 centimetres (8 inches) thick. Interestingly, until 1790 shoe-makers did not make different shoes for the left and right foot – they used the same model for both feet.

Even if you cannot make it to Alicante, you may be lucky enough to see some of the museum's holdings in one of its travelling exhibitions. One of these is the fabulous 'The Shoe through Nature', which includes footwear modelled on the four seasons, the four elements, fauna and flora. There are intricate designs in the shapes of swans or mice, shoes embellished with scorpions, and boots painted with underwater scenes. Other designs are influenced by the arts and architecture: Picasso's *Guernica*, or the Roman aqueduct of Segovia.

And every year for Christmas the museum constructs a nativity scene entirely made out of shoes, plus a Christmas tree decorated with festive footwear.

THE FROG MUSEUMS

Grabenackerstrasse 8, Münchenstein, CH-4142, Switzerland
Telephone: (Switzerland 0041) (0)61 373 0830
www.froggy.ch

and

Musée Communal, 13 rue du Musée, Estavayer-le-Lac,
CH-1470, Switzerland
Telephone: (Switzerland 0041) (0)26 663 2448
www.museedesgrenouilles.ch

'Frog, n. A reptile with edible legs.'
Ambrose Bierce, *The Devil's Dictionary*, 1911

Like so many specialist museums, the one at Münchenstein started as a private collection that swelled to enormous proportions. It all began with a single pewter frog bought in Germany in 1981. A year later, Elfi Hiss and Rolf Rindlisbacher had 500 frogs.

In 1992 they had to move their 5,000 frogs from Basel to their present location, where they installed them in a handsome new museum in a craft centre. Since then the collection has almost tripled in size.

The frogs are made out of ceramics, wood, glass, crystal, plush, paper, plastic and even chocolate. There does not appear to exist a household object that can't be froggified. From shoes to thimbles, watches, magnets and bottles, they are all here in their full green glory. The fame of the collection continues to spread. Nearly 700 enthusiasts travelled to the museum's ten-year Jubilee in 2002.

On the website a friendly green frog chirrups a welcome. It links to interesting frog sidelines, like the 75th anniversary of the carnival in Lucerne, commemorated by the erection of 75 large polyester frogs over a metre high in the town centre.

Switzerland is big enough for two very different frog museums. There's another at Estavayer-le-Lac, on the shores of Lake Neuchâtel. This museum contains 108 stunning examples of historic frog taxidermy, with the specimens taking part in satirical tableaux of daily life 150 years ago: in the schoolroom, in the kitchen, at a tavern, in battle. The plump pale frogs are equipped with miniature furniture and accessories. They feed tiny chickens, pour themselves glasses of wine, play poker at a table in a tavern, go to the barber's and dress up as soldiers, fully armed.

The frogs were collected in the mid-19th century by a Swiss Guards officer, Monsieur Perrier. His preservation technique was to extract their innards through their mouths and then fill the empty bodies with sand. How he managed to preserve their delicate skins is still a mystery. Still more so is the way in which Monsieur Perrier created a different facial expression in every individual frog.

'If it is originality you are seeking, you won't be disappointed', promises the museum's website. The same museum, in an atmospheric stone building, hosts a collection of items from the Bronze Age and lacustrian period, some historical weapons, the uniforms of Swiss mercenaries who fought in the Burgundy Wars, and a collection of lamps and railway signals.

Meanwhile, in California another frog enthusiast, Pamela S. Livingston, hosts the www.califrognia.com website, another rich source of imagery and information.

And for the true frog fanatic, there's the House of Frog Museum in Kirksville, Missouri, and the Annual Frog Collectors' Convention held at the Frog Fantasies Museum in Eureka Springs, Arizona (www.frogfantasies.com). This collection, started in 1937, probably boasts the most venerable pedigree in America, and contains at least 7,000 frogs.

Amsterdam has a Frog Museum too, at Frederik Henriklaan 38. It's open the first Sunday of each month, to show its collection of over 5,000 frogs.

THE MUSEUM OF HOAXES

Online at www.museumofhoaxes.com

'Free baby boy to good home. My ex-girlfriend had him a few weeks ago, but now he just sits in my closet and cries. I'm not too sure how to deal with it, and I'm in a pretty low financial spot. I lost all the baby accessories. Batteries not included. Transaction final. No returns. Guaranteed not DOA.'

This special offer was posted on Craigslist, an online classified ad service, and is typical of the items 'curated' by scientist Alex Boese on the website he started in 1997. The idea grew out of a doctoral dissertation that was never finished. Boese's superb website, in contrast, has grown to an impressive depth and receives at least a million hits a month. Online contributors and Boese's own beady eye keep the site constantly refreshed with new outrages and idiocies, and cast light on old ones. It's also a useful place to check up on the latest internet scam.

The Museum of Hoaxes examines each new dubious photograph that appears on the internet, tracing Photoshop scams back to their original constituents and even praising the creativity of some computer hoaxers.

Like a real museum, the 'exhibits' are classified and archived. In the historical wing, hoaxes are presented chronologically, starting with the Middle Ages and the female pope and the Scythian lamb, or vegetable lamb. Part plant and part animal, this creature took the form of a lamb rooted into the ground by a thick stem that grew from its belly. It could eat only the grass that grew near it.

There's a Gallery of April Fool's Day hoaxes, with the top spot going in 1998 to the *Babil* newspaper, owned by Saddam Hussein's late son Uday. In different years, Uday variously informed his readers that President Clinton had decided to lift sanctions against Iraq, or that bananas, Pepsi and chocolate would be added to their food rations. Later, *Babil* explained that these were in fact just very funny jokes. On similar lines, the Gallery of College Pranks features a press release issued at Columbus in 1993 to announce a new charity for the homeless. Instead of food and shelter, this charity aimed to provide guns and ammunition, and went by the name of 'the Arm the Homeless Coalition'.

The Tall-Tale Creature Gallery features such mythical monsters as the Coydog and 'the Beast of Balbirnie', which turned out to be a straying St Bernard dog. Boese exposes the latest Nigerian begging scam, which offers gullible animal-lovers an expensive chance to save a bulldog puppy. He tracks down instances of frogs allegedly packed in bags of salad around the world. He explodes the notion that mice love cheese, and debunks the more obscure one that cows moo with regional accents. The bonsai kittens grown in glass jars are soon dismissed. As are the meat-flavoured dog condoms.

But truth is often stranger than fiction. Other creatures that seem to be fake are in fact real, such as the fur-bearing lobster, the liger (half-tiger, half-lion), the glow-in-the-dark deer, and the horned rabbit known as a jackalope. It is also true, apparently, that the urinals at Amsterdam's Schiphol airport all bear an etching of a fly in the bowl, as men automatically aim at it and splashing is thus avoided.

The virtual visitor can submit to a test of his own gullibility. Questions include: 'Marco Polo introduced ice cream to Europe after watching it being made in China – true or false?' And there's a hoax photo test to check up on your visual and detective skills.

'Hoaxpert' Alex Boese has authored two books, *The Museum of Hoaxes* (Dutton, 2002) and *Hippo Eats Dwarf: A Field Guide to Hoaxes and Other B.S.* (Harcourt, 2006).

THE TITANIC MUSEUM

208 Main Street, Indian Orchard,
Massachusetts 01151-0053, USA
Telephone: (USA 001) 413 543 4770
www.titanichistoricalsociety.org

'The concerted cry of despair that came from the direction of the
liner as she plunged into the ocean is ringing in my ear this minute
… It sounded like a mighty wail, co-mingling the hoarse shouts of
the men and the shrill screams of the women.'

The sights and sounds from the
lifeboat described by survivor Dorothy Gibson

I t's the small things that bring home the tragedy of the *Titanic* – small, humble objects carried away by survivors fleeing the sinking vessel. There's no logic to what people grabbed as they fled. This in itself gives a sense of the panic and unreality of that tragic night in 1912, when the so-called Unsinkable sank to the floor of the North Atlantic Ocean, taking 1,496 souls with her. The Titanic Museum in Indian Orchard contains the finest collection of *Titanic* artefacts assembled before the discovery of the wreck itself. Since most of them were supplied by survivors, there's a very personal touch.

There's a menu from third-class passenger Tom Theobald. A saloon steward, Frederick Dent Ray, saved a remnant of carpet from a first-class stateroom. New bride Selena Rogers Cook, in second class, contributed a tooth that had ached on the journey. There's Milton Long's pocket-watch and Mrs John Jacob Astor's lifejacket. There are the buttons of Frank Goldsmith, whose autobiography *Titanic Eyewitness, My Story*, is the only personal account of the disaster written by a third-class passenger.

The *Titanic*'s look-out Frederick Fleet sketched the fatal iceberg – that haunting document's here too, as is the Marconigram ice warning from SS *Amerika* – donated by the wireless operator himself. The shipbuilders Harland and Wolff have given an original blueprint of the design of *Titanic*'s lowest deck. There's a handwritten account by survivor Gershon 'Gus the Cat' Cohen of his ordeal, written while aboard the *Carpathia*, the vessel that saved him. He was called Gus the Cat because he avoided several fatal accidents during his life.

The Titanic Historical Society runs the museum. It's a global organisation with more than 7,000 members. The society produces a quarterly magazine, the *Titanic Commutator*, named after the ship's instrument that measures the tilting of a vessel. This was the first instrument that Captain Smith consulted when he arrived on the *Titanic*'s bridge after the collision with the iceberg.

The *Commutator* has been in print for more than 40 years, and each issue unearths new accounts from survivors, such as the film star Dorothy Gibson, who recalled that there was a great deal of merriment on board on the night of the disaster. She was playing a lively game of bridge when she felt 'a slight jar'. Nothing was said to the passengers, who only gradually noticed the nervous behaviour of the stewards. In the surge of passengers towards the lifeboats, she remembered the 'greenish paleness' of Bruce Ismay, chairman of the White Star Line that owned the *Titanic*, and how the lifeboat needed to be plugged with voluntary donations of lingerie from the female passengers.

A 2.75-metre (9-foot) model of the *Titanic* dominates the displays in this small museum. Three-dimensional models show the functioning of the ship's engines, rudder and propellers. Other exhibits demonstrate the very different ways of life on board for first-, second- and third-class passengers – comparing, for example, the crockery used in the various dining rooms, and also the accommodation and conditions for the officers and men.

In some ways this museum is more evocative than the hi-tech displays that have been created since the *Titanic*'s wreck was located. There is perhaps more romance contained in these objects from a time when the great ship and its demise were almost mythical. Now that the wreck has been found, charted, filmed, and Hollywooded, one almost loses sight of the human dimension to the story. This museum brings it back.

Amid all the tragedy there's one happy artefact: the death certificate of *Titanic* steward J.E. Puzey. The General Registrar Office of Shipping and Seamen issued the document dated 20 June 1912. His grieving family was delighted when it turned out to have been issued in error. Steward Puzey turned up unharmed at the family home.

THE CARROT MUSEUMS

Berlotte, Eynatten, Belgium, and online at
www.carrotmuseum.com.

'Large, naked, raw carrots are acceptable as food only to those who live in hutches eagerly awaiting Easter.'

Fran Lebowitz

I've said it elsewhere in this book, and I'll say it again: the Belgians really know how to enjoy themselves. Witness the Carrot Club and Museum of Berlotte, founded in 1992.

Only men are admitted. But they manage to have a damn good time all the same. Wolfgang Hillen, the treasurer and secretary, explains: 'Our club goals are to contribute to society happenings and to make jokes or silly things … Our working life is serious, so we need in that club fun for our life.'

The Carrot Museum was erected in an historic electricity substation that dates back to 1910, a time when the area was open countryside. The 20th century has not spoilt this once entirely rural area. Wolfgang Hillen reminisces: 'You can remember the farm life, because often there is much shit on the road.'

You visit the tiny museum only from the outside. Through a window, the visitor beholds a wheel that moves the display around to show all the exhibitions serially. On the exterior, there's a tower with a carrot clock, carrot weathervane and carrot light.

This modest museum is not to be confused with the all-singing, all-dancing virtual carrot museum at www.carrotmuseum.com. This site is devoted to the culture and history of the carrot, and there's an illustrated section on 'carrotabilia', including Limoges carrots, carrot fans, carrot teapots, etc. There are also links to famous carrot collectors, such as the incomparable Romana, who runs the Armistead Cottage B&B in Rhode Island, USA. Photographs of the cottage show what is probably the finest and largest collection of carrots in the world. Visitors even stay in the Carrot Room (55 Hunter Avenue, Newport, RI 02840, telephone: (USA 001) 401 848 7123, email: Romana or Charles @Armisteadcottage.com).

Meet Greg Warren, who grows carrots that he styles into romantic works of art and then photographs before eating. And the Norwegian collector who commissioned a carrot-shaped guitar.

On this site you can see reproductions of the carrots featured in the works of the old masters. Modern art is not neglected: see the 5-metre (17-foot) 'Soft Sculpture Carrot' by Lauren Jackson in San Diego. And in Rochester, New York, there's the *Carrot Wheel* installation, a biodegradable work of art. The curators explain that in order for the composition to remain intact, the carrots need to be replaced regularly, resulting in a different concept of 'worth'.

www.carrotmuseum.com offers so much more! There's an addictive carrot face-maker – you can drag eyes, noses and mouths and hats from a selection over to a central carrot and create a unique face for it. You can find out about the carrot festivals held in Holtville, California, and around the world. Learn about the Beta-Sweet, a sugary maroon-coloured carrot. See the Flutenveg, the musical duo from Western Australia. They play instruments carved out of carrots.

And for all those tricky carrot questions ... you can ask Mr

Carrot on curator@carrotmuseum.co.uk – that is, in the unlikely event that they aren't already answered by the awesome list of carrot facts in the trivia section or his scholarly history of carrots. For example, did you know that the longest carrot ever recorded was in 1996 and measured 5.14 metres (almost 17 feet)? Or that Howard Hughes measured every carrot he ate? After reading this site, you will also learn that the Anglo-Saxons used carrots medicinally, against the devil and insanity, and that the Greek soldiers who hid inside the Trojan horse were said to have consumed raw carrots to suppress their bowels.

THE MUSEUM OF WEIRD
CONSUMER CULTURE

Online at www.indiana.edu/~wanthro/museum.htm

'Consume: to take up completely ... devour, waste, destroy, spend.
To cause to disappear or vanish away. To destroy a living being, or
more usually a race or tribe by any wasting process. To spend goods
or money, especially wastefully.'

A definition posted on the museum website

This online museum names and shames gross examples of the consumer culture. For example, who *really* needs neuticles, fake testicles for dogs so they won't experience a sense of loss after castration? Or the solar-powered cappuccino frother? Or the special bloodshot-effect contact lenses for Hallowe'en?

The museum is a part of a website created by Rick Wilk, professor of anthropology at Indiana University and past president of the Society for Economic Anthropology. Other pages of his site include a directory of novels on the theme of poverty and a satirical list of ridiculous new jargon words to describe globalisation, for the use of those in the business of it.

The Museum of Weird Consumer Culture is the most entertaining part of the site. Its aim is to expose 'the most banal, grotesque, ironic, twisted or perverse creations of the capitalist marketplace'. 'Exhibits' in its virtual halls go back to the earlier part of the 20th century, when 'the American Way' started to be way too self-confident – or could that be rapacious and dominant? This is the question posed by Professor Wilk: 'Is American culture covering the earth like a blanket of paint? Does everyone in the world wear Nike and eat at McDonald's? Is the planet going to become one big shopping mall, full of people who listen to the same music and watch the same movies?'

The answers are fairly devastating. In 1987, as the site reports, the number of shopping centres in America exceeded the number of schools. The average time spent shopping per week is six hours. The minutes spent playing with children per week: 40. The amount of time the average American will spend watching TV commercials: one entire year of his or her life. Only 8 per cent of people in the world own a car; 89 per cent of American households have one or two.

Other astonishing statistics: The number of Americans with two or more homes tops 10 million. Americans account for 5 per cent of the world's population, but consume 30 per cent of its resources. By the time a baby born today in the United States reaches 75, he or she will have created 52 tons of garbage, been through 43 million gallons of water and used 3,375 barrels of oil. The amount of energy used by one American is equivalent to that used by three Japanese, 38 Indians, 168 Bangladeshis or 531 Ethiopians.

Since 1940, Americans alone have used up as large a share of the earth's mineral resources as all previous generations put together. And a final statistic to bemuse the visitor: eight out of ten Americans regard themselves as 'environmentalists'.

These same environmentalists are the customers for the products curated in the museum – a satellite dish for campers, electric baby-wipe warmers, etc. Not all the products are American. There's 'Virgin Pink' nipple-lightening cream from Japan and bizarre examples of American clothes, beverages and lifestyle seeping into distant world cultures. Much is lost in translation.

While there's much fun in mocking absurd products, this site also explores alternative, less greedy ways of being. There's a 'Living Lightly' section with advice and anecdotes. Posted online there's a thought-provoking sample course on the spread of consumer culture. This signposts the environmental impact of conspicuous consumption in the developed nations, and the uglification and flattening out of their cultures into a lifestyle founded on status anxiety, mass-produced goods, shopping malls and celebrity worship.

And does our material luxury actually make us happy? Apparently not. The rise in per capita consumption in the USA in the last twenty years amounts to 45 per cent, yet the quality of life, according to those polled, has decreased by 51 per cent.

THE KOMBOLOI [WORRY BEAD] MUSEUM

25 Staikopoulou Street, 211 00 Nafplio, Greece
Telephone: (Greece 0030) 27520 21618
www.komboloi.gr

'The komboloi is the companion of many in their daily and lengthy communion with God, and of others, in longer or shorter moments, in their lesser or greater joys, very often in the unbearable ache of their loneliness …'

Aris Evangelinos

*K*omboloi, or worry beads, originated with the Muslim religion at least 1,400 years ago. The faithful used tightly-strung beads to count off their sequence of prayers. Turkish conquerors brought the beads to Greece. In the hands of the Greeks, the strings of beads became looser. This allowed the owner to move them along the string, making a companionable little click as one bead struck another. The beads are relaxed in another way as well: in Greek culture, the *komboloi* are now recreational and soothing rather than religious. Other cultures still use beads to count their prayers and appreciate the metaphor of a necklace as a never-ending cycle of prayer. Hindu and Buddhist faiths have their 'worry' beads. And, of course, the Catholic rosary developed in parallel and for a similar purpose.

'Kombo' means 'knot' but it has an older significance too – the sound of two hard objects knocking together, like beads shuffled along a string. 'Oi' means a line of similar objects. 'Leo' can also mean 'I say'.

At the age of fourteen, an Athenian boy named Aris Evangelinos became fascinated with the amber-yellow worry beads clicking in his grandfather's hand. He began to ask questions and was introduced to a colourful new world, that of the collector of *komboloi*. It was the beginning of a lifelong passion. After inheriting his grandfather's superb collection, Aris Evangelinos began his own quest, amassing *komboloi* from all over Greece and the East. On his journeys he collected as many stories and friendships as garlands of beads. His *komboloi* were made from bone, horn, coral, ivory, mother-of-pearl and crystal, though the classic ones are always amber.

Aris Evangelinos eventually settled in the old fortified town of Nafplio on the Peloponnesian coast. In 1998 he turned his collection into a small private museum with exhibits dating from 1750 up until the present time. He also published a beautiful illustrated book, *The Komboloi and its History*, which is as much about his own personal history as that of the *komboloi*, the two being completely interwoven on a spiritual and emotional level.

An 18th-century building hosts the collection. A workshop on the ground floor produces worry beads for sale, as well as handmade jewellery, charms, amulets and keyrings. The upper floor houses the historical collection, along with explanations of the provenance and meaning of different kinds of *komboloi*. Some *komboloi*, like those from Mount Athos, feature 30 or 50 knots instead of beads. There's a Buddhist necklace known as *mala*, meaning prayer. There are 108 prayers on a Buddhist *mala*, and the beads are flat discs of bone, decorated with silver and bronze.

But it's the modern Greek usage of the *komboloi* that must still be the most appealing. How much more pleasing than the constant fondling of mobile phones, and the obsessive fingering of Blackberries, is the Greeks' way of quietly clicking their beads, whether in the car, the café or walking along the street. The discreet charm of the *komboloi* is that it disentangles worries instead of tightening them.

THE PASTA MUSEUM

Piazza Scandenberg 117, near the Trevi Fountain,
00187 Rome, Italy
Telephone: (Italy 0039) 06 699 1119 / 699 1120
www.museodellapasta

'Everything you see I owe to spaghetti.'   Sophia Loren

Pasta is often said (by ignorant non-Italians) to have come to Italy from China, brought back by the Venetian merchant-traveller Marco Polo. Not so! Rome's Museo Nazionale delle Paste Alimentari comprehensively refutes this slander. Important documents dating as far back as 1154 prove without a shadow of doubt that pasta was already being made during the 12th century in as many as four different regions of Italy. Moreover, new archaeological evidence suggests that even the ancient Romans may have enjoyed a plate of *pasta al pesto*.

So let us put an end to this wicked myth of non-indigenous pasta by asserting its true history – an Italian pedigree that the Pasta Museum is not ashamed to repeat, reinforce and re-emphasise. Inside the museum 'you will discover eight centuries of the national "first course", the Italian invention that the world envies us!'

The visitor proceeds through eleven rooms spread over two floors, after which there will be almost nothing about pasta left to learn. Not only are the manufacturing processes explained in detail, but the techniques of pasta cooking in the home are revealed. The Rubino-Scaglione room focuses on the relationship between pasta and art, including the theatrical arts – there's even a theatre made out of pasta.

You'll also learn that pasta was originally eaten with the fingers, not with forks. This is illustrated with scenes of Italians happily cramming spaghetti into their mouths without the aid of cutlery.

The different kinds of pasta are displayed, from the universally known *penne* to the more picturesque types with even more evocative names, such as *creste di galli* (cocks' combs); *ziti* (bridegrooms – lightly curved tubes, up to 30 centimetres (12 inches) long); *occhi di passero* (sparrow eyes – discs with little holes); and *mostaccioli* (little moustaches). Not to mention *strozzapreti* (priest-stranglers, which look like rolled-up towels – apparently the ideal tool for this essentially Italian occupation).

Serious documents from pasta history are also exhibited with suitable solemnity. The museum sponsors an annual prize for contributions to pasta studies.

With Italy's claim to pasta invention firmly established, the museum also waxes evangelical. Pasta could become the national dish of every country, the museum explains – much to the economic and nutritional benefit of the whole world.

In the shop, the visitor can buy pasta postcards, pasta posters, pasta cookbooks and pasta gadgets. Actual pasta is also for sale, in the form of 'la pasta del museo' – a box of samples in ten different shapes.

Given the patriotic nature of this museum, the visitor won't be surprised to find that all the display boards are in Italian, but audio-guides are available in English, Spanish, French, German and Japanese.

It is an interesting historical footnote that Italy's rampant futurist movement turned against pasta. In *The Futurist Cookbook*, published in 1932, various Italian writers and artists of the avant-garde poured spicy scorn on the national dish. Libero Glauco Silvano condemned pasta in tomato sauce: 'This dish, surely more bestial than any other, looks to us like a female chimpanzee in a sentimental ladies' drawing room.'

And 'Futurist Aeropainter Fillia' ranted: 'Pasta is made of long silent archaeological worms which, like their brothers living in the dungeons of history, weigh down the stomach ... You mustn't introduce these white worms into the body unless you want to make it as closed, dark and immobile as a museum.'

The National Cowgirl Museum and Hall of Fame

1720 Gendy Street, Fort Worth, Texas 76107, USA
Telephone: (USA 001) 817 336 4475
www.cowgirl.net

'As a child I always had a fondness for adventure and out-door exercise and especial fondness for horses which I began to ride at an early age and continued to do so until I became an expert rider being able to ride the most vicious and stubborn of horses, in fact the greater portion of my life in early times was spent in this manner.'
The Life and Adventures of Calamity Jane
(Martha Jane Cannary Burk), 1896

America's cowboy culture spawned many household names, but the great women of the prairies and pampas have remained, with rare exceptions, unknown.

Yet those gutsy gals who shaped the west changed the world. They endured physical hardship, flouted conventions, fought for their lives. They deserve a break. That's what the good folks think down Fort Worth way, where America's cowgirl tradition is properly celebrated, Texas-style, with the very latest in museum technology peppered with over 5,000 historical artefacts, including saddles, spurs and clothes. As they say in Texas, enjoy the ride!

Outside the museum, a massive bronze sculpture, *High Desert Princess*, greets the visitor. It's the work of Mehl Lawson, member of the Cowboy Artists of America. And on the façade, a Richard Haas mural of cowgirls gallops straight towards you.

Inside, your visit starts with the 'Spirit of the Cowgirl Theatre'. A film shows the many faces and roles of the historical and modern cowgirl – young, old, rodeo stars, artists, ranch women, mothers.

Hi-tech rules the ranch in the Hall of Fame inside the first-floor rotunda. A dozen murals made of optical glass shift to show different images as the visitor passes – cowgirl portraits morph into images of cowgirls at work. 'Honorees' of the cowgirl tradition are named on a ribbon of etched glass stars known as 'the Spirit Trail'. Their stories are told electronically in two large touch-screen 'yearbooks'.

'Into the Arena' allows visitors to recapture the excitement of famous female wins in great races. In the Arena Style section, flamboyant rodeo fashions are displayed on a mechanised rack controlled by a touch-screen panel that explains the life of the women who wore these chaps, split skirts and cowboy hats. Interactive doesn't come much more physical or sophisticated than the Cowgirl Museum's bronco-riding experience. The museum will film your performance, composite it into an old-style rodeo scene, speed up the action and post the whole spectacle on their website for you to download at home. Visitors can also pose for a portrait to be superimposed on a movie-poster setting. The image is then available as a postcard-size print.

The Claiming the Spotlight section contains blown-up images of the many glamorous movie stars who have played cowgirls, from the fearsome matriarch Barbara Stanwyck to the honey-tongued 'Queen of the West' Dale Evans. In a recreation of an old-time theatre, a film narrated by the actress Katherine Ross chronicles the lives of the Hollywood cowgirls, from stunt doubles and damsels in distress to gun-toting dames. She's interrupted sometimes by a talking horse head above the stage. (Forget the women, he wants to talk about the role of horses. *Far more important, dude.*)

Meanwhile an original 1950s television set shows clips from *Annie Oakley* and *The Roy Rogers Show*, and jukeboxes warble country and western classics by Patsy Montana, the original 'Cowboy's Sweetheart', Patsy Cline and Reba McEntire.

In the gift shop you can also buy cowgirl hats, rhinestone cowgirl belts, pecan pies and even a cowgirl razor. Those gals really knew how to live!

The museum opened in 1975 in Hereford, Texas, before moving to Fort Worth in 1993 and the current premises in 2002. Only part of the vast holdings is on show: the museum maintains in its research library an invaluable collection of photographs, films, diaries, biographies, historical recollections and oral histories.

THE MUSEUM OF THE SEWERS OF PARIS

Near 93 quai d'Orsay, 75007 Paris, France
Telephone: (France 0033) (0)1 5368 2781
Email: Visite-des-egouts@paris.fr

*'The sewer is the conscience of the city. Everything there converges
and confronts everything else. In that livid spot there are shades,
but there are no longer any secrets. Each thing bears its true form,
or at least, its definitive form. The mass of filth has this in its favour,
that it is not a liar ... A sewer is a cynic. It tells everything. The
sincerity of foulness pleases us, and rests the soul.'*

Victor Hugo, *Les Misérables*, 1867

Victor Hugo believed passionately that all the waste of Paris
should be recycled to fertilise the land and feed the
starving. 'A sewer', he pronounced, 'is a mistake.'

The rulers of Paris thought otherwise, and thanks to them
there's not only modern plumbing in the city but also a very
special tourist attraction, a place where the imaginative visitor
can relive the desperate adventures of Jean Valjean, Hugo's protagonist, scurrying through the highly metaphorical filth and
darkness deep at the heart of the City of Light. Paris is well
known as a gourmet destination, but the other end of the
alimentary canal gets the royal treatment here too.

What Hugo called 'the Intestine of Leviathan' dates back to
the 13th century, when it consisted of open trenches. It was first
covered over by Napoleon. In the 1850s a complex programme
of sandstone tunnels was undertaken. The sewer canals of Paris
today stretch for more than 2,400 kilometres (1,490 miles) in

135

circuitous routes under the city, carrying effluent to treatment plants. They also host water pipes, communication cables, rats and spiders. The public parts of the Parisian underbelly are now visited by technical professionals, film-makers and 90,000 tourists a year.

Sewer tourism is nothing new to Paris. The first public visits were organised for the 1867 Universal Exhibition, after Baron Georges-Eugène Haussmann revolutionised and purified the system. By popular demand, they continued. At one time, tourists could view the sewers from carts suspended from the walkways, and later there were tours on a locomotive every last Saturday of the month. Between 1920 and 1975, boat tours were available. These days, tourists take a dry, secure foot-route through a representative 500-metre (1,600-foot) section of the vast network, beneath the quai d'Orsay on the Left Bank.

Guided tours are free when available; English tours are offered only in the summer. But independent viewing is easy, using the free booklet issued with the entrance ticket.

The visitor first descends to a long gallery parallel to the Seine and 5 metres (16 feet) below street level to inspect a vast 'flushing boat', a waste-water filter and grit chamber. Then one crosses a footbridge to reach a feeder-sewer that leads to the main exhibition area, the Belgrand Gallery. This is below the sewer that leads to the École Militaire.

What's on show: a documentary film on life in the sewers; an exhibit tracing the history and design of the sewer and many physical artefacts, such as the huge wooden balls used to clear the cylindrical pipes; models of a dredger boat and sewer workers in their rubbery uniforms; and a stuffed sewer rat of impressive dimensions. There's a fresco of Jean Valjean carrying his limp burden and a reconstruction of his route. Most of all, there's *atmosphere* – the great stone caverns, humid air and, at times, a little whiff of history, ancient and modern.

The gift shop sells T-shirts, postcards and copies of Hugo's *Les Misérables*, with its incisive commentary on the sewers not just of Paris but of the world. Let us give the last word to Mr Hugo, ironically the best apologist for a visit: 'Crime, intelligence, social protest, liberty of conscience, thought, theft, all that human laws pursue or have pursued, have hidden in this hole.'

Now it's your turn. And by the way, this is one museum where there's no café.

THE MUSEUM OF JURASSIC
TECHNOLOGY

9341 Venice Boulevard, Culver City, California 90232, USA
Telephone: (USA 001) 310 836 6131
www.mjt.org

*'In its original sense, the term "museum" meant a spot dedicated
to the muses – "a place where man's mind could attain a mood of
aloofness above everyday affairs."'*
      Museum of Jurassic Technology's introductory comments

Most modern museums set out to make order from abundance. The Museum of Jurassic Technology instead seeks
to be extremely solemn about a number of seemingly unrelated
and bizarre objects. The sensation of someone pulling hard on
your leg is sometimes hard to ignore as you wander through the
crypt-like gloom of its interiors and peer at its elegant display
cases. For this is a museum that gently satirises museums, that
seeks to unbridle the visitor's thoughts instead of shepherding
them into a tidy corral.

The Museum of Jurassic Technology preserves the flavour of
the eccentric private museums of the past – 'a flavour which has
been described as "incongruity born of the overzealous spirit in
the face of unfathomable phenomena"'.

The visitor's you're-having-me-on-ometer should start to
twitch on learning that the museum claims to document the
technology of the 'Lower Jurassic', a period that had no technology. Only geology. And dinosaurs, of course.

So the exhibits are designed merely to bemuse and perplex the ordinary visitor and to titillate the irony-receptors of the highly sophisticated.

David Wilson, an avant-garde film-maker, is the *éminence grise* behind this museum. Wilson has been awarded a MacArthur 'genius' fellowship, reserved for scientists, artists and dreamers of true creative status. His museum is for people, like himself, who prefer the road less travelled and enjoy the roadside attractions thereon.

That includes the intellectual adventurer Athanasius Kircher, honoured with several galleries for his inventions and discoveries. He shares museum space with, for example, the Old World or Asian quail. ('The female is generally duller in colour than the male, which is already markedly dull.')

The stink ant of the Cameroon merits an inclusion because of its pitiful life cycle. As this ant forages for food it frequently inhales the spores of an insidious fungus of the genus *Tomentella*. The fungus sends the ant into a frenzy. It climbs high into the forest, digs its mandibles into a branch, and waits to die. Meanwhile the *Tomentella* devours all the soft tissue of its host, and eventually projects a spike out from what was once the unfortunate insect's brain. This spike grows to 3 centimetres (1.5 inches) in length. Its bright orange tip is loaded with spores … that drop down to the forest floor and infect more stink ants, with the same unpleasant and fatal consequences.

'The Horn of Mary Davis of Saughall' grew out of the back of the poor woman's head. It's noted that men who grow horns usually display them at the front of the head, whereas women's horns tend to be at the back. This specimen, from around 1688, is 15 centimetres (6 inches) long. (Miniature versions are available as earrings in the gift shop, alongside T-shirts that read 'Dispirited after a Dreary Day with the Prospect of a Depressing Morrow'.) Then there's the Deprong Mori or Piercing Devil of the Tripiscum Plateau in South America, alleged to be able to pierce through hard objects.

The Borzoi Kabinet Theatre screens *Levsha: the Tale of a Cross-eyed Lefty from Tula and the Steel Flea*, drawn from the 'beloved mid-19th-century novella' by Nicolai Semyonovich Leskov ...

The Garden of Eden on Wheels features a selection of mobile home and trailer parks in the Los Angeles area. The museum also shows some of the micro-miniatures of Hagop Sandaldjian, who created sculptures inside the eyes of needles. Among his masterpieces are a tiny Napoleon and a Pope John Paul II.

The Old Operating Theatre

9a St Thomas Street, London SE1 9RY, England
Telephone: (UK 0044) (0)207 188 2679
www.thegarret.org.uk

'The glory of surgeons is like that of actors, who exist only in their lifetime and whose talent is no longer appreciable once they have disappeared.' Honoré de Balzac

The oldest surviving operating theatre in Europe does indeed resemble a quaint miniature stage, with tiers of standing-only places rising up above it. The operating table itself is a simple deal plank. The instruments look like something from a child's toybox (if a rather sadistic child). It's only when the smiling curators call down volunteers from the audience to re-enact an early 19th-century amputation, minus anaesthetic, that the visitor starts to conceive a real sense of the grim past of this place.

And theatre is the right word for it. Doctors were not paid for the lives they saved, but by the students who crowded in to watch them at their skilful butchery. Given the lack of sanitation, the breakneck speed of the surgery and the primitive aftercare, mortality rates were unsurprisingly high at around 20 per cent. At one stage, patients being admitted to St Thomas' Hospital were asked for their funeral expenses in advance.

The attic operating theatre was walled up in 1862 and rediscovered only by chance a hundred years later, so it's in pretty much the original condition. It has been refurnished with original equipment from the correct period.

Modern visitors climb the spiral stone staircase up to the garret which houses the herb and instrument collection that now abuts the old surgical space. The theatre itself was built high up, above St Thomas' Church, in order to catch as much natural light as possible. There was no such thing as surgical lighting in those days. Post-operative patients were lifted on a hoist across to the ward block, now the London Bridge post office. Via the same door, unlucky patients were hoisted down to the morgue.

In those pre-anaesthetic days, it was probably a good idea to have the sounds of screaming somewhat removed from the street. It could take up to an agonising hour to remove a bladder stone via an incision near the anus. Amputations were usually over in less than a minute, mercifully.

Now, outside the theatre, in what was once a women's ward, are collections of bone-chilling surgical instruments, such as the cranioclast, used to crush the heads of dead babies inside the womb to make their extraction easier. There are sets of surgical knives, saws, bleeding bowls, cupping jars and a number of anatomical specimens, including the skeleton of an extraordinarily large male hand.

The curator, Karen Howell, is an expert in pharmacological history and has gathered together not just the artefacts of medicine but also examples of the herbs, so you can touch and smell garlands of the real dried plants that festoon the dark beams. Attend one of her fascinating lectures and you'll learn about the connections between ancient Egyptian religion, apothecaries and modern medicine. She will explain the more unusual exhibits such as St Thomas' Hospital's own recipe for snailwater (a popular 'cure' for syphilis in the 18th century), a stuffed crocodile and a real human brain.

The mice which used to devour the curator's poppy heads have been banished by sonic plugs in a recent refurbishment, but the atmosphere remains truly, scarily Dickensian. Poetry readings and theatrical performances are occasionally held at this unique museum, and are not to be missed by anyone who enjoys a good fright.

WOLF SONG OF ALASKA

PO Box 671670, Chugiak, Alaska 99567-1670, USA
Telephone: (USA 001) 907 688 9653
www.wolfsongalaska.org

'Befriend this magnificent symbol of wildness.'
Tom Talasz, executive director

It's not everyone who can visit this impressive Alaskan centre dedicated to saving the disappearing wild wolf. But via the website you can literally befriend 'the magnificent symbol of wildness' – by adopting a wolf long-distance.

Tom Talasz explains: 'Our adoption programme allows you to express your awareness of the plight of the wolf and helps to further the public's understanding and acceptance of this magnificent and often misunderstood species.'

The wolf adoption package includes a photograph by the internationally acclaimed wolf behaviourist and wolf photographer Monty Sloan, and a certificate, suitable for framing. The certificate can be personalised with any name of your choice. As Tom Talasz suggests, you can even adopt a wolf for your own dog or cat back home, not to mention any particularly deserving colleague, friend or family member.

Wolf Song of Alaska was established in 1988. The museum is arranged in a series of dioramas that bring the great outdoors of Alaska indoors. The visitor wanders through autumn forests and snowy winter days on the tundra. There's a constant reminder that you have ventured into wolf territory: a soundtrack of their howls echoes through the building.

The first part of the visit takes you to the Predator-Prey area, showing wolves stalking moose, oxen and other animals. The next stop is the Pack Behaviour zone, where you learn about wolf 'scent rolls', the way they use eye contact to communicate, and their courtship behaviour.

Visitors are taught about the wolf's natural history, its relationships with humans through the ages, and its role as a major symbol in human folklore, art and religion. Wolves, you may be surprised to hear, are a very friendly species, given to displays of affection between family members and averse to aggression. A behaviourist has observed a wolf distressed by a fight between two dogs, to the extent that it grabbed the tail of one of the combatants and dragged it away.

The website looks into medical matters, such as hypertrichosis, a condition that causes excessive hair growth over the face and body. Through history people afflicted with this condition have been called werewolves or wolf-children, and often ended up in circuses and freak shows.

Wolves feature strongly in literature, right up until modern times. In the human subconscious, wolves are associated with freedom, independence and something both wild and sacred. In recent years, wolves have become literary fashion items: Clarissa Estes' bestseller about female self-empowerment, *Women Who Run with Wolves*, was succeeded by Pam Keesey's anthology, *Women Who Run with Werewolves*.

To adopt a wolf, go to www.wolfsongalaska.org/adopt_wolf. html.

Wolf Song merchandise (including Christmas decorations, camisoles and baby bibs) is available from the museum store,

The Alaska Wolf Cache, from the website and also online at www.cafepress.com/wolfsong.

THE SZABÓ MARZIPAN MUSEUM

Dumtsa Jenö u. 12, H-2000 Szentendre, Hungary
Telephone: (Hungary 0036) (06)2 631 1931
www.szamosmarcipan.hu

'I prefer to regard a dessert as I would imagine the perfect woman: subtle, a little bittersweet, not blowsy and extrovert. Delicately made up ...'   Graham Kerr

This is Hungary's original marzipan museum, and suitably situated in a sweetly picturesque little town where baroque architecture rhapsodises quaintly with the Bohemian, in both senses of the word. From the 1920s, the little town, 19 kilometres (12 miles) north of Budapest, was a flourishing artists' colony. Today it hosts a number of folk museums, of which the most remarkable is the Marzipan Museum.

The museum is dedicated to the life and work of the outstanding Hungarian confectioner, Mátyás Szamos. His life in marzipan began with a rose. An ethnic Serb, the fatherless young Szamos was living in poverty in Szentendre in the 1930s when a famous Danish pastry-chef came to town and demonstrated how to make beautiful roses from marzipan. The little boy, whose sweet tooth was probably inherited from his Balkan ancestors, was hooked. He trained as a confectioner, married into a confectionery family, and founded a marzipan dynasty and a company that today employs over 200 people.

The museum exhibits sculptures, artworks, paintings and decorations manufactured from sugar, chocolate and, above all, marzipan. It's quite amazing what can be conjured from just three basic ingredients – almond paste, egg white and sugar, plus a bit of food dye and a lot of skill.

You'd expect this museum to be 'sweet' and it doesn't disappoint, but this is high-kitsch, ranging from the solemn to the tongue-in-cheek.

Among the masterpieces on display: a life-size chocolate statue of Michael Jackson (*What* are little boys made of???) – and a portrait of Princess Diana. Also featured are great leaders from Hungary's colourful past. There's a 160-centimetre-tall (5-foot) model of the parliament building; a tableau of the whole Flintstone ménage; the whole cast of *Sesame Street*, including a genuinely wistful Kermit and a lush Miss Piggy; a basket of puppies with their toys and even their messy bowl of dog food; village scenes with apple trees; and a whole herbarium of utterly convincing exotic cacti and flowers. Also a tableau of Ali Baba surrounded by minarets, and the cast of *The Wizard of Oz*.

There's even scary marzipan, in the shape of a sabre-toothed, pop-eyed dark dinosaur.

It's almost a relief to see that there is marzipan used for its original purpose – cakes. A wedding cake lacy as a bridal gown is topped with flowers … made from marzipan. Another stands as tall as a man. There's a beautifully intricate carriage spun of white sugar and inlaid with painted panels.

The museum is small, immaculate and colourful, draped with royal blue curtains. On the first floor, you can watch the marzipan sculptors and painters at work behind giant windows, using the same utensils as their forebears a hundred years ago.

Nearby is the original confectionery works, still a thriving business. In the elegant ground-floor café and shop are sweets to be eaten or taken away. The beautiful room has terrazzo flooring and walls decorated with majolica tiles. Upstairs is a function room decorated with reproductions of the paintings of Gustav Klimt.

THE MEGURO PARASITOLOGICAL MUSEUM

4-1-1 Shimomeguro, Meguro-ku, Tokyo 153-0064, Japan
Telephone: (Japan 0081) (0)3 3716 1264
www.kiseichu.org/english.aspx

'Try to think about parasites without a feeling of fear …'
Akihiko Uchida, former director, from the museum brochure

The curators of this quintessentially Japanese museum faced up to a basic problem head-on. The fact is that parasites, by their very nature, make their homes deep inside the living bodies of other organisms. If the host animal dies, then the parasite dies too. It has therefore been impossible for the curators to show their star exhibits alive and in action.

Never mind – the museum has taken a creative approach to this issue, with a slick multimedia presentation: diagrams, maps, models, books and etchings, and yes, of course, the odd disgusting parasite preserved in a glass bottle. The museum's captions are in Japanese, but an excellent colour booklet (costing £1.72/400 yen) explains the exhibits in detail. The pitilessly clear diagrams speak for themselves …

The museum was originally set up as a research facility privately endowed by Satoru Kamegai, a doctor of medical science. It's still a charitable, non-profit organisation and doesn't charge admission, though donations are welcome. Behind the scenes at the museum, there's intense research and publication activity, and constant acquisition of new specimens.

Here are some sobering facts – there are over 70,000 parasite species, and over 6 per cent of all animals are parasites. The museum showcases 300 examples.

Naturally, the museum's attitude to parasites is on the positive side. The curators point out that only unsuccessful parasites kill the hosts that sustain them. So many are harmless, if unwelcome, guests.

Some parasites are species-specific; others roam from host to host. The 'definitive' host is the one in which the parasite comes to its sexual maturity and lays its eggs. That's a million eggs a day, in the case of the tapeworm, by the way. The museum hosts a specimen that is 8.8 metres (29 feet) in length. The museum's brochure explains helpfully: 'Although there are no apparent symptoms once infected, a person recognises the disease when the worm hangs from the anus during defecation.'

Worldwide, around a hundred parasites have been identified in humans. Other species seem to be more attractive to the parasite brethren. One exhibit shows a profusion of noodle-like parasites (filarial nematodes) bursting from the heart of a dog. In another bottle sits the large intestine of a flying squirrel, stuffed full of pinworms. As the museum's brochure notes: 'With so many pinworms, the flying squirrel must have had quite an itchy derriere!'

Of course, some parasites are dangerous to humans. Plasmodium, the malaria parasite, causes destruction of human red blood cells. Roundworms infested 70 per cent of Japan's population after the Second World War. The squirrel's problems seem quite minor compared to those of the man depicted in a painting by Hokusai Katsushika. Filarial worms in his lymphatic vessels have given him elephantiasis of the scrotum. The victim is forced to carry his afflicted organ in a sack hung from a stick. Bigger than his entire torso, the scrotum is so heavy that he needs a friend to help him lift it.

THE MUSEUM OF QUESTIONABLE
MEDICAL DEVICES

The Science Museum of Minnesota,
120 West Kellogg Boulevard, Saint Paul,
Minnesota 55102, USA
Telephone: (USA 001) 651 221 9444
www.smm.org www.mtn.org/quack

*'The museum is the world's largest display of what the human
mind has devised to cure itself without the benefit of either scientific method or common sense.'*   Bob McCoy, proprietor

Picture this as a cure of constipation. You set yourself down on a rather ornate wooden chair with a hard wooden seat and a padded cushion for your head. The operator plugs the chair in. The chair begins to vibrate violently. You feel a sharp pain in your lower regions. The chair goes on jolting you until one of the doctors at the Battle Creek Sanitarium releases you from your agony, assuring you that your body's own peristaltic motions, now accurately stimulated, will take care of the rest of the business. How could it fail?

Dr John Harvey Kellogg and his brother Will Keith Kellogg ran Battle Creek, a world-famous health resort during its heyday in the early 20th century. One of their diet innovations, Kellogg's Corn Flakes, has survived them, but the Vibratory Chair was not to prove a bestseller. Instead, it now takes pride of place in the Museum of Questionable Medical Devices, alongside the Recto-Rotor, the Prostate Gland Warmer and the Vital Power Vacuum Massager, designed to help the user 'be a manly man'.

This museum of medical outrages grew out of the private obsession of one man, Bob McCoy, who set out to collect the physical artefacts, advertising and legal history of quack medicine. He accumulated over 400 devices – some unscrupulous frauds, others the triumph of honest hope and ignorance over true science.

Mr McCoy has also dissected the methods of the quacks to explain why they have been so successful over the centuries. The cleverest medical con-artists showed amazing creativity and an understanding of human insecurities. The best marketing ploy is to invent a problem, or 'medicalise' a normal bodily process, such as menstruation, into a serious health issue – for which he or she (there have been many female quacks) just happens to have a revolutionary and safe solution.

Another 'quack' technique is to claim that the proprietary device or medicine cures an enormous range of illnesses, thus craftily increasing the market share. The Heidelberg Electric Belt, for example, boasted in its advertising that it cured 'weakness in men and women, personal exhaustion … impotency, rheumatism, sciatica, lame back, railroad back, insomnia, melancholia, kidney disorder, Bright's disease, dyspepsia, disorders of the liver, female weakness, poor circulation, weak heart action and almost every known disease and weakness'.

Some of the machines in this collection are still in working order, and visitors may even submit themselves to a phrenology reading. The victim dons a huge helmet that measures all the bumps on the head, each one indicative of personality traits like intelligence, spirituality and sexual continence.

You can also see court judgements against proven frauds and

posters for products that have fortunately not survived. There's a beautifully illustrated advertisement for a most extreme form of diet pills. Eat 'sanitised' tapeworms, this scam suggested, and they would eat the food in your stomach and you'd lose weight!

The Vibratory Chair and tapeworm pills seem ridiculous to modern eyes, but people these days are just as gullible as their grandmothers. Just give us a bit of pseudo-science, a long word, a model in a white coat and glasses – and a bit of hope – and we're happy. There's a foot-operated Breast Enlarger Pump, vintage 1976: millions of women bought it. There's also the Toftness Radiation Detector, confected out of PVC piping and couplings, to rub over the back of the patient. The practitioners claimed that neurological damage in the spine manifests itself in emissions of radiation.

Bob McCoy originally housed his collection in St Anthony Main, Minneapolis. On his retirement in 2002, he donated his entire collection to the Science Museum of Minnesota in St Paul, where a selection of exhibits can now be seen. The website illustrates and explains a wide range of the items and makes a fascinating read.

The Hall of Flame Museum of Firefighting and National Firefighting Hall of Heroes

6101 East Van Buren Street, Phoenix,
Arizona 85008-3421, USA
Telephone: (USA 001) 602 275 3472
www.hallofflame.org

'Sometimes I almost feel sorry for the education folks at other museums, because we've got what kids want to see – cool old fire trucks. Unless you've got dinosaurs, we've pretty much got you beat with the under-ten crowd. Every year hundreds of kids pass through here on field trips, and I can't remember ever seeing a bored face on any of them.'

M. V. Moorhead, curator of education at the Hall of Flame

It's true – almost an acre of fire engines! All lovingly tended and restored, many in working order, and each with a story to tell.

Like the Brush Model D, a magnificent work of art with a one-cylinder engine and wooden frame and axles. This 1909 engine was the pride and joy of the fire chief of Owensville, Indiana – until one humiliating day in 1920, when he was over-taken by a little boy on a bicycle who was in a hurry to see the fire. The Brush Model D went into retirement shortly afterwards.

Fire engines in the museum date from 1725 to 1969. Most of the engines are American, but there are pieces from England, France, Austria, Germany and Japan. Exhibits include fire apparatus, artwork, uniforms, helmets and equipment, alarm room technology, a fire-safety demonstration house, and many hands-on displays for children. There are speaking trumpets once used by fire chiefs to direct their companies to fires. Best of all, visitors can climb aboard the American La France Model 700 engine from 1951, donated by the city of Miami.

The museum was the brainchild of George F. Getz. In 1955 his wife gave him a most unusual Christmas present – a 1924 American La France fire engine. A collection was born. Six years later it had its own small museum, and by 1974 it had moved to its current premises in Phoenix, with six exhibit galleries, a library, a store, a theatre and a restoration workshop.

It's not just hardware, it's social history; as curator M. V. Moorhead explains: 'In a sense, the history of civilisation is the history of firefighting.' Fire was once the scourge of all cities, causing death and destruction on an unimaginable scale. Only in 1720 did American towns start to set up fire teams of volunteers. Sometimes there was fierce rivalry about the equipment, which changed dramatically over the years from horse-drawn and pedal-powered to steam, to automotive.

By 1925 nearly all fire engines were motorised. Hoses, helmets and ladders all moved with the times too. Warning systems have moved from rattles and bells to hi-tech electronics. Extinguishing liquids developed from water through poisonous carbon tetrachloride to liquorice-based Foamite and beyond. A fireman of 1890 would have been stunned to see the technology available to his counterpart a hundred years later.

Some carriages in the museum were almost purely decorative, for use in parades. Others were proper workhorses, like the

Autocar High Pressure Fog Engine, circa 1950, that served for 27 years in the Philadelphia suburb of Ardmore, during which time it made more than 8,000 runs.

Smoke kills more people than fire. The greatest innovation in firefighting was the development of breathing equipment that allows firefighters to enter burning buildings. Sprinklers have also saved many lives. The museum mentions more than once a sobering fact: no one has ever died from fire in an American home equipped with an operating sprinkler system.

In 1998 the museum opened the National Firefighting Hall of Heroes, honouring Americans decorated for firefighting heroism and those who died in the line of duty. Visitors can use a computer to read the stories of all those honoured here.

In 2004 the gallery received a donation of a full-size model of a quarter horse to honour the firefighters and policemen who died in the Twin Towers. The painted horse was a gift from a public arts project called the Trail of Painted Ponies (www.trailof paintedponies.com). Poignantly, beside the memorial pony lies a fragment of the World Trade Center's rubble.

THE GERMAN BUTCHERS' MUSEUM

Marktplatz 27, 71032 Böblingen, Germany
Telephone: (Germany 0049) (0)7031 669473 / 669485
www.boeblingen.de/Fremdsprachen/Englisch

'Let the stoics say what they please, we do not eat for the good of living, but because the meat is savoury and the appetite is keen.'
Ralph Waldo Emerson

The sausage is the star of this serious three-storey museum that recounts the history of the German butcher, a powerful figure in folk legend, fairytale and of course on the high street.

For where, as this museum explains, would the German be without his butcher shop? It was in the 15th century that specialist shops selling cuts of meat and fine sausages first started to appear in Germany, and they soon became the focal point of not just culinary but social life in towns and villages.

True to that tradition, the German Butchers' Museum is housed in a beautiful half-timbered mansion right on the market square of Böblingen, a picturesque, dynamic town south of Stuttgart. This elegant establishment claims the honour of being the only German museum devoted to the historic world of butchers and butchering.

Within its walls are loving recreations of butchers' shops from the 14th century to the recent past: a butcher shop from 1860; an example of a sausage kitchen from around 1900; a country butcher's shop from 1920. Each is equipped with all the contemporary tools of the trade and original artefacts of interest and charm. Looking at the majolica counters, the painted ovens, the elegant tiles, one starts to get an idea of the importance of the butchery trade in the sociological and cultural development of Germany.

A serious and – truly! – attractive exhibition takes the visitor through the history and techniques of the German butchery trade, including slaughtering and meat processing.

Further exhibition areas are dedicated to the guild history of the butcher business. A guild room with its shop, flags and documents evokes the glory days of the guilds. Newly opened showrooms in the *Vogtsscheuer* (bailiff's barn) deal with nutrition and the role of spices in the preparation of meat.

Sausages, dried meats and festive cuts form the backbone of the German diet and have naturally got the creative juices flowing in more places than the kitchen. The top floor of the museum houses a fascinating exhibition of works of art featuring meat and butchers at work. There are porcelain figures of butchers and their beasts, still-life paintings, delightful folk art and medieval woodcuts. A cheerfully urbane model pig poses cross-legged in an upholstered armchair. There's even a Beryl Cook painting of a satisfied and happy pig sunning himself in the branch of a tree.

Until the end of the 20th century, the museum hosted the Böblingen *Schlachtfest* (slaughter party). Put aside fantasies of blood fountains and throat-cutting at once! The *Schlachtfest* was a sedate affair during which the butchers presented their sausages on long tables for tasting. On the stage, the experts gave speeches about the handicraft and science of sausage-making and new horizons in sausage-cooking. Butchering celebrities also made guest appearances, and the audience was entertained with music and by comedians as they chatted, danced, and of course, consumed sausages. It was, we are reliably informed, just an amusing evening for like-minded carnivores.

THE MUSEUM OF TORTURE AND
MEDIEVAL CRIMINOLOGY

Via del Castello 1/3/5, Piazza della Cisterna,
53037 San Gimignano, Toscana, Italy
Telephone: (Italy 0039) 0577 942243
www.torturamuseum.com

*'The reasoning behind it ran something like this: "We torture you,
and if you are innocent God will intervene and halt your suffering,
otherwise He will be happy to see you suffer."'*
Curator and scholar Aldo Migliorini, on Inquisitional torture

San Gimignano's torture museum was the first of many
devoted to the revolting devices of coercion and punishment
that have shamed the human race for centuries. There are torture
museums in the German cities of Freiburg and Rothenburg ob
der Tauber, in Prague and many other places. However, this
museum has an advantage over all its rivals, being situated in an
atmospheric medieval town of looming towers and narrow
alleys, where, on dim evenings, it is easily possible to imagine
oneself back in times when the screams of torture victims
echoed over the soft Tuscan hills.

And indeed the message of this museum is precisely for now.
Should one visit torture museums? Aldo Migliorini explains that
the shock of seeing these cruel instruments forces the visitor to
think about violations of human rights that continue today. The
more one ignores such violations, the more likely it is that they
will continue. 'Torture should be exposed because silence makes
us accomplices, and possibly victims.'

The San Gimignano museum is an authentic anthology of horrors. Many of its exhibits date from the time of the Inquisition when torture was institutionalised and codified. The rack was the Inquisition's device of choice, allowing progressive torture. But more 'creative' tools were available too. Bizarrely, they were often given picturesque names.

Here's a brief sampler: dreadfully heavy 'necklaces' for ne'er-do-wells (or slackers in church attendance); the maiming stork (on which the victim was pinioned, doubled-up); the Judas cradle (a sharp pyramid onto which the victim was forcibly lowered); the expandable oral, rectal and vaginal pear for lechers; the knee-splitter; the skull-crusher; the breast-ripper; the Spanish spider for hooking victims through their skin; the cat's paw or Spanish tickler for ripping flesh; and the elongated spoon for pouring molten lead into human orifices.

There's a grim Gothic example of a spiked Inquisitional chair, used in Europe right up until the 1800s. San Gimignano's specimen has 1,300 spikes. The maiden of Nuremberg was an upright sarcophagus topped by a carved woman's head. The door was fitted with spikes designed to pierce different parts of the body without causing death, though enough time inside it would certainly result in a lingering, painful end. Speaking of maidens, there's a beautifully crafted Venetian chastity belt that mortified the flesh of the wearer.

The garrotte was a pole with a rope that was tied around the victim's neck. The rope would be wetted so that it would shrink, causing slow suffocation. A Spanish version used a steel collar with a spike that penetrated the vertebrae.

Not all instruments killed. Branks were an instrument of

humiliation as well as torture. These metal face masks were fitted with long asses' ears or even pig snouts. The victim's mouth, nose and eyes were stoppered up, and screaming was impossible. The shrew's violin was a portable pillory.

A touring section of the museum's holdings travels around the world, and has been seen in San Francisco, Buenos Aires, Tokyo and many European cities.

THE MUSEUM OF DEPRESSIONIST ART

Online at www.dearauntnettie.com/museum
Telephone: (USA 001) 503 323 3259

'Absolute heresy! Sets the art world back a good five or six decades.'
Unpaid reviewer who wishes to remain anonymous

According to its creators, Ernie Jurick and Ditty Nicolaides, the Museum of Depressionist Art came about as an antidote to those tedious, large art books filled with unctuous prattle about 'angular linearity', 'effective plasticity', 'surging elation of brushstrokes' and similar twaddle 'penned by artsy types who can't hold honest jobs'.

This museum's specific field, Depressionism, is a hitherto undiscovered school of painting 'that permeates the art world like a heavy coat of brown varnish, treating artists and works normally overlooked by your average hoity-toity art books'.

For one thing, the museum's artists are largely fictitious, and the works, although real enough (and some of them genuine classics), have been modified sufficiently to avoid the need to pay licensing fees to the 'craven, grasping descendants of the original artists'.

An excellent example of the school of Depressionism is Edvard Monk's delightful *Office Xmas Party, London Society of Morticians,* 1905. Monk, best known for his diptych, *Despairing Figure on the Bridge/Despairing Figure no Longer on the Bridge,* in this masterpiece reveals the private side of the usually grim and dour undertaking profession as they miserably celebrate the holiday in a garret over a funerary supply store.

Among landscape artists, the outstanding Depressionist is Halcyon Le Brume, whose 'fogscapes' in even tones of grey manage to eliminate every detail from the Breton coastline he used as a model. Le Brume was born before the invention of the paint roller, with which he could have turned out twenty or thirty masterpieces a day. Thus are great masterpieces lost to the world.

The 19th-century limners of the American frontier also have a home in Depressionism. The aptly named 'American Primitive' – a naive, unknown artist – created hundreds of works which survive today. His or her work is readily identifiable by the presence of a huge cat's head occupying most of the painting's visual space. This device can be intriguing, as in *Landscape with Cardinal, Passenger Pigeon and Enormous Cat Head*, but it becomes somewhat distracting in historical subjects like the artist's *Washington Crossing the Delaware with Troops and Enormous Cat Head*, which looks like the bastard offspring of the well-known Leutze work and something by René Magritte.

The museum is virtual only, as the city refused the curators a building permit on the grounds of irrelevance.

There are several hundred works by an assortment of artists in the Museum of Depressionist Art. Those with the stamina for it are invited to investigate the Gallery of the Unidentifiable annexe of the main building, filled with sculptures and other items which take up more space and are therefore harder to ignore than paintings.

THE PABLO NERUDA HOUSE

La Sebastiana, Ferrari 692, Valparaíso, Chile
Telephone: (Chile 0056) 32 225 6606
www.fundacionneruda.org

I gave myself over to the cheapest doors,
Doors that had died
And had been pitched out of their houses ...
And I said, 'Come
To me, lost doors.
I will give you a house and wall
And a hand to knock on you.'

Pablo Neruda, from 'To la Sebastiana'

The incomparable Chilean poet and diplomat Pablo Neruda lived a life rich in imagery, and he filled his homes with objects that inspired him.

Neruda's left-wing politics often forced him into hiding or exile. His death from cancer, twelve days after Pinochet's military coup in 1973, was seen as symbolic of the country's fallen state. The murdered president, Salvador Allende, had been Neruda's dear friend. Soon afterwards the Nobel laureate's homes were plundered and vandalised.

Fortunately the houses have been restored by the Pablo Neruda Foundation, set up in 1986 by Matilde Urrutia, Neruda's third wife and constant muse.

Perhaps the most interesting of Neruda's homes is La Sebastiana. The rickety building hovers like a ghost ship high above the glorious city of Valparaíso. The azure waters of the old port glitter in every window, and the eye follows the roofs of Valparaíso's rainbow buildings down to the shoreline. Those same colours suffuse La Sebastiana's interior walls.

Neruda adored Valparaíso. In 1959, he first saw the ramshackle collection of stairs and terraces perched on Florida Hill. The original owner, a Spaniard named Sebastian Collao, had begun construction with pipe dreams of heliports and an entire third floor designed as a birdcage. Collao died before the building was finished.

Neruda persuaded his close friends Marie Martner and Francisco Velasco to buy the property with him. They would take the lower storeys; he would occupy the third and fourth floors and the tower. It took three years for Neruda to finish the house to his satisfaction. The 'casa Sebastiana', as the poet christened it, was itself the subject of a delightful poem in which Neruda explains how it was constructed of found materials.

One of the first things Neruda hung up was a portrait of the American poet Walt Whitman. One of the builders asked Neruda if the old man was his father. Neruda replied: 'Yes, in poetry.'

La Sebastiana was launched, as she was to live, with a great party. Each guest was honoured in an 'unforgettable merits list'. Neruda always liked to spend New Year's Eve in Valparaíso, watching the fireworks.

The house was restored in 1991 and opened as a museum thanks to the support of Telefónica de España, which also made possible the acquisition of the lower part of the house. A walk through La Sebastiana is like a meander through the poet's mind. Curators have ensured that every visitor can get the most from each battered and eccentric object, with leaflets in many languages to make the connections between objects in the house and Neruda's captivating work.

The house is still suffused with the poet's playful spirit. In the living room there's a stuffed coro-coro bird encased in a glassy bubble. A horse from a Parisian merry-go-round rears up nearby. Off the living room there's a satirical little bar (where Neruda mixed his deadly Coquetelon cocktail). Upstairs in his study, there's a beautiful painted sink that Neruda never plumbed in: a metaphor in which the poet apparently revelled.

Neruda spent his last year at La Sebastiana. Francisco Velasco recounted that soon after the poet's death he arrived there to find everyone in turmoil. Cautiously, he climbed the stairs to investigate. He found an enormous eagle in the living room. 'Immediately, it came to my mind that time when Pablo confided that if there was another life, he would have liked to be an eagle', wrote Velasco.

Neruda had three houses in Chile: La Sebastiana in Valparaíso, La Chascona in Santiago and Isla Negra.

THE MUSEUM OF AUTOMATONS

4, rue Anne-Marie Javouhey, 11300 Limoux, France
Telephone: (France 0033) (0)6 7039 0174
www.limoux-aud.com/lesmusees

'I have always been fascinated with imaginary people. In the beginning I made them in an attempt to find my mother who disappeared when I was thirteen months old and whom I tried to recreate, in my own way, from bits of information that I gleaned here and there. I also had, as a child, a strong urge to make inanimate things live; to make my puppets and dolls come alive.'

Martine Morand, creator and curator

Enter the Museum of Automatons and you will feel something eerie in the air. There's a fluttering of silk. A whisper of gauze. A flashing of painted eyes. The glitter of a spangle.

In the high-ceilinged entrance hall, a number of life-size and larger-than-life-size figures welcome you, bowing and waving. From here you pass into a large gallery and all heaven is let loose. Baroque music fills the air. The walls are draped with ruched gold. More than 200 figures, decked out in lace, silk and sequins, curtsey, turn from side to side or make subtle gestures with their hands and heads. Some are turbaned, some masked. You feel as if you have suddenly gatecrashed an extraordinary fancy-dress party.

Most of the figures seem lost in their enchanted worlds, with faraway looks in their eyes. This strange and wonderful party is attended by creatures of all sizes: waiters, pierrots, fairground ladies, fortune-tellers. There are ghostly transparent figures draped in wisps of silver; cat faces on human heads.

The museum is a monument to one couple's lifelong passion for the art and technology of automatons. Martine Morand and Jean-Jacques Achache searched for many years for a perfect site for their museum. Finally, they settled on the town of Limoux, once famous for its shoe industry. An abandoned shoe factory has been restored to their own design and now houses both their collection and their workshop, which opened as a museum in 2006.

Martine and Jean-Jacques have worked together for over 30 years. She's from Sarlat in the Périgord, and studied at the École des Arts Décoratifs in Paris. Jean-Jacques, of French colonial stock (*'pied noir'*), lectured at the École Technique des Arts Graphiques et Photographiques in Toulouse.

Every piece in the museum was made by the couple. The 'gestation' of a particular character may take a long time, but the actual making is intense and happens over a short period of perhaps only a week. Rigorous research into contemporary images and documents goes into the creation of each figure, but Martine and Jean-Jacques admit that so much of themselves goes into each character that what emerges is always a completely new individual. Jean-Jacques, who is responsible for the mechanics, works hard to achieve a realistic movement.

In the best tradition of small museums, the visitor can talk to the creators about their work here. The couple are keen to stress that their art has no philosophical pretensions. If anyone cares to find a message, that's their business. This lack of theorising means that the artists are able to switch from creating Puss-in-Boots one minute to working on some mysterious Venetian carnival figure the next. And this is one reason why the automatons are not labelled or 'curated'. The intention is that each visitor should have his or her own experience of the automatons.

A child once whispered to Martine that the characters had truly come to life, that she had taken them away, and that they had continued to live with her. That is exactly what the artists hope will happen.

MISTER ED'S ELEPHANT MUSEUM

6019 Chambersburg Road, Orrtanna,
Pennsylvania 17353, USA
Telephone: (USA 001) 717 352 3792
www.mistereds.com

'When you've got an elephant by the hind legs and he is trying to run away, it is best to let him run.'   Abraham Lincoln

Most people get dinnerware or silver as a wedding present. Ed Gotwalt was given an elephant figurine. And you know how it is with elephants. You get one, and your bride thinks it's looking a bit lonely one day, so she gets you another one. You happen across another couple on your honeymoon. Then word gets round that you collect elephants and suddenly every birthday and every Christmas unleashes a stack of elephants upon you. You build a few shelves. Then an annexe for your elephants. Before you know it, you have 6,000 elephants and you have to start calling your collection a museum.

According to Ed Gotwalt, elephants are natural collectors' items for humans, as the two species have so much in common: 'Elephants take care of each other, as do most humans.'

This is the only museum of pachyderm memorabilia in the world. Mister Ed, as he's universally known, opened it in 1975, not far from the famous Gettysburg battlefield. Mister Ed, like his favourite beasts, is somewhat larger than life. Bearded, jovial, sporting a chunky gold elephant on a chain round his neck, he talks non-stop elephant. If he's on the premises, he'll happily talk you round his collection. His elephants are not 'curated' or captioned. They simply stand there, in their thousands. So a sentimental journey with Mister Ed will add a great deal to your visit. His own closest encounter of an elephant kind, as he'll tell you, was when he rode a circus animal down the main street when it came to town.

Mister Ed has a host of non-pachydermal anecdotes too. A one-time actor, showman and shopkeeper, he never forgets a good story from any of his past lives. When he ran a general store, his annual appearances as Santa were the stuff of legend, involving mobile log cabins and Belgian mares. He once decided to arrive by hot-air balloon, only to crash into a tree along the way.

What you'll see in the museum: a vintage 1940s elephant hairdryer, an elephant potty chair, an elephant pulling a 24-carat gold circus wagon, elephant clocks, teapots, jewellery, an elephant telephone, and a bizarre sculpted head from Mexico with elephants leaping out of it. There are elephants blown from Murano glass, carved from oyster shells, fashioned out of banana leaves.

What you won't see is anything made from modern ivory. Naturally, Mister Ed abhors the cruel trade. 'Only elephants', he maintains, 'should wear ivory.'

'Shoplifters will be trampled', says the sign in the candy and gift shop. To refresh yourself after your elephantine exertions you can sample Mr Ed's famous Jumbo Peanuts, which are prepared in his vintage roaster. Visitors to the museum consume 30 tons of peanuts a year. They also buy beaded elephants, elephant desk accessories and real ostrich eggs painted with elephant motifs.

Mister Ed fell into peanut production rather in the way he

fell into pachydermania – by chance. However, there is at least one correspondence. 'Elephants', he says, 'love peanuts. I've fed them many over the years. They eat them shell and all.'

Visitors can pose for pictures with Miss Ellie Phunt, a life-size fibreglass elephant, who is wired up to wriggle her ears and chat with the visitors about the changes in the seasons and the smell of peanuts roasting nearby – and she'll advise them to make their way along to the museum or gift shop. Miss Ellie and Mr Ed are immortalised together in the store's snow-globe, a snip at $5.98.

THE ICEMAN MUSEUM

South Tyrol Museum of Archaeology,
Museumstrasse 43, 39100 Bolzano, Italy
Telephone (Italy 0039) 0471 320120
www.iceman.it

'And yet there is a solitude which each and every one of us has always carried with him, more inaccessible than the ice-cold mountains, more profound than the midnight sea: the solitude of self.'
Elizabeth Cady Stanton, address to Congress, 18 January 1892

On 19 September 1991, German hikers trekking in the Ötztaler Alps made a gruesome discovery: a set of human remains frozen in a melting glacier. It seemed that they were looking at the victim of a murder, possibly a hiker like themselves. They could not have guessed the whole truth. The Iceman had indeed been murdered. At the time he was probably about 46 years old. He was 1.55 metres (5'2") in height. He'd quite recently eaten some cereal and venison. But the really unusual thing about the man found in the glacier was that he had lived and died at least 5,300 years ago.

When scientists examined the etiolated corpse they were astonished. And the unknown man was soon an international celebrity. Despite the millennia that had passed since his death, the ice had kept both the man and his clothes in such an excellent state of preservation that he was able to yield up clues about his life and times that had never before been available to archaeologists. And not just to archaeologists: anatomists, pathologists, anthropologists and many other 'ologists' were excited about the discovery, and what it had to teach them.

Ötzi, as he was nicknamed, was found in the Alps that border Italy and Austria. The two nations at first squabbled over his provenance and final resting place. It was proved, however, from the contents of his stomach, that Ötzi hailed from the Italian side of the Alps. And so the body of the Iceman can now be seen by the public at Bolzano's South Tyrol Museum of Archaeology, set up in 1998 to house both Ötzi and a wealth of other artefacts that document life in the area from the end of the last Ice Age (15,000 BC) until around 800 AD. The museum, in a handsome former Banca d'Italia building, shows its collection chronologically, so the visitor walks in sequence through the Stone, Copper, Bronze and Iron Ages up to Roman times and the Dark Ages.

Ötzi now lives at a steady temperature of −6°C (−21°F) in a sophisticated refrigeration unit with a viewing window for the public. The humidity is set at 99 per cent, and a unique thermo-conservation process stops the body from dehydrating, while preserving as closely as possible the climatic conditions of the glacier where the Iceman spent his last 5,000 years. One of the reasons for his perfect preservation was the fact that he lay buried under the ice in almost complete darkness. The museum has solved this problem by using 'cold light' and a special system of filters to avoid ultraviolet radiation.

There's a life-size model of Ötzi as he would have looked. He wears a thick grass cape, a bearskin cap, goat-hide coat and leather shoes, and carries the copper axe with which he was found, along with a fairly impressive array of other weapons.

Ötzi is the most important 'document' to the life and times

of the Copper Age. His axe, for example, bears testimony to the fact that humans had already mastered metal technology five millennia ago. The blade of the axe was cast in a mould. It was fixed onto a wooden shaft with leather ties and birch tar. Examination of the Iceman's body shows that he himself worked with smelted metals.

Studies continue apace into the Iceman, his life and his death. Recently it has been suggested that he died of his wounds after hand-to-hand combat. An arrow has been found embedded in his shoulder. He probably bled to death.

Meanwhile, like that other famous corpse, Tutankhamen, Ötzi's myth has expanded to embrace his own modern-day 'curse'. Seven people loosely related to the discovery and study of the Iceman have succumbed to untimely deaths from causes such as an avalanche, a fall, a car accident and from a heart attack.

Ötzi has been the star of *Mnemonic*, a fascinating play created by Simon McBurney of the renowned Complicité theatre company. McBurney, the son of an archaeologist, traces the discovery and the competing theories about the Iceman, taking him as a symbol for the essential humanity that has not changed in 5,000 years.

They Also-Ran Gallery

First State Bank, 105 West Main, Norton,
Kansas 67654, USA
Telephone: (USA 001) 785 877 3341
www.firststatebank.com

'Politics is a recurrent dream – there is no cure.'
Horatio 'The Know-Nothing Candidate' Seymour,
Democrat presidential hopeful for 1868

You could never say that Henry Clay didn't take a shot at the presidency of the United States of America. Clay, also known as 'the Cock of Kentucky', was a presidential candidate for *three* different parties, the Democrats, the National Republicans and the Whigs. Between 1824 and 1848, Clay was a vigorous contender and a vitriolic campaigner for the top job – and consistently lost.

Henry Clay's haughty face takes its place in this unusual museum, housed in the mezzanine of the First State Bank in Norton, Kansas. His companions are other notable losers like General Winfield Scott (aka 'Old Fuss and Feather') and Aaron Burr. Neat ranks of wooden-framed photographs line the walls. Under each portrait there's an explanation not just of the political history of each candidate but also his position on such issues as slavery. The museum takes a fascinating look into the campaigning style of the aspirants and the quality of their oratory.

Attacks on the opposition could get very personal. Winners were not exempt. President Lyndon Baines Johnson once joked:

'I am making a collection of the things my opponents have found me to be and, when this election is over, I am going to open a museum and put them on display.'

Extra personal flavour comes from the candidates' nicknames and famous word-bites associated with them. Thomas Jefferson, author of the Declaration of Independence, for example, was known as 'the Sage of Monticello'. And Wendell L. Wilkie, Republican candidate in 1940, was heard to explain an extravagant promise made in a speech thus: 'Oh, that was just campaign hooey.' (He promptly lost to Democrat Franklin D. Roosevelt.)

It's interesting these days to note how many presidents and aspiring presidents were supplied by America's military establishment. Winfield S. Hancock ('Superb Hancock') ran for president in 1880 after spectacular success on the battlefield. Abraham Lincoln had written of him: 'When I open my mail of a morning, I do so with fear and trembling lest I hear Hancock has been killed or wounded.'

The museum was set up 42 years ago by W.W. Rouse, former owner and president of the First State Bank. Mr Rouse, a devoted history buff, was inspired by Irving Stone's 1964 book, *They Also Ran*, an account of unsuccessful contenders for the American presidency.

Horace 'Old White Coat' Greeley is considered the museum's greatest Also-Ran. Born the third child of a bankrupt farmer, Greeley rose to fame as a politician and journalist, founder of the *New York Tribune*, supporter of Abraham Lincoln – and failed presidential candidate in 1872. He lost to the Republican General Ulysses S. Grant. Greeley is said to have stopped in Norton while on the campaign trail. And this small historical detail was what inspired the banker Mr Rouse to start putting together his collection of the not-quite-great and the not-always-good.

Not all the Also-Rans ended up in obscurity, however. Some were comeback kings, like Stephen Grover Cleveland, who returned in triumph after being defeated for a second term. Some of the Also-Rans ended up as winners or lost their bids for re-election. Presidents such as John Adams were defeated, sometimes more than once, before they claimed the ultimate prize.

Knife-edge election results are nothing new in America. The museum reminds visitors that Democrat Samuel Jones Tilden received the majority of votes in 1876 but ceded to Rutherford B. Hayes when the Republicans disputed the returns.

The museum is constantly updated, with Al Gore and John Kerry lately immortalised in the ranks of Also-Rans. The current curator, Lee Ann Shearer, says: 'To my knowledge, there is not another gallery like ours.'

THE FOX-GOD TEMPLE

(Fushimi Inari Taisha, Fushimi Inari Shrine)
68 Fukakusa Yabu-no-uchi-cho, Kyoto 622-0882, Japan
Telephone: (Japan 0081) (0)75 641 7331
www.inari.jp (in Japanese)

'For a good life: Work like a dog. Eat like a horse. Think like a fox.
And play like a rabbit.'
George Allen

This beautiful temple featured in the most memorable scene of the film *Memoirs of a Geisha*. The young heroine Chiyo runs up through its extraordinary passageways to leave her offering for the god, in the hope that she might escape her wretched existence as a servant and become a glamorous geisha.

Ten thousand pairs of shrine gates (*torii*) arch over a long pathway stretching 4 kilometres (2.5 miles) up the hill behind the main shrine complex. These gates are painted in glorious foxy colours – vivid orange and black. They are so closely spaced as to appear a solid wall from a distance. Each of the gates was donated by people and businesses grateful to the god for their prosperity, and is inscribed with personal and professional messages.

In fact, the shrine, dating back to 711 AD, is really dedicated to the Shinto deity, Inari, who protects the rice harvest, rice farmers, rice merchants and the general prosperity of business, as well as that most important rice product – sake. The fox (*kitsune*) is Inari's messenger. Most images of the god (sometimes shown as a goddess) are flanked by two foxes. The foxes apparently outgrew their patron in popularity and are often

182

depicted on their own. They are certainly dominant here – pairs of stone fox statues guard the entry to each of the site's shrines.

Inari's foxes are generally benevolent beasts in Shinto mythology. They are said to be helpful, but others are said to be dangerous and inclined to bewitch people, sometimes posing in the guise of a beautiful woman. Foxes are also believed to be capable of possessing human souls by entering the body under the fingernails.

All around the temple there are huge statues of grinning foxes, some equipped with microphones. If any child attempts to climb up the statue, the stone fox intones: 'Please do not climb the statue. It may be dangerous.' Some of the foxes have large keys in their mouths – these represent the keys to the rice granary that they protect.

Restaurants near the temple serve *kitsune udon* ('fox udon'), a noodle soup topped with pieces of fried tofu, said to be considered a delicacy by foxes. When the temple celebrates its festival in February, sweet fox-shaped rice crackers (*kitsune senbei*) are always on sale for the hungry pilgrims. At this time, thousands of businessmen come to the temple to ask for their ventures to be blessed by Inari and her foxes.

THE PEANUTS MUSEUM

(The Charles M. Schulz Museum and Research Center)
2301 Hardies Lane, Santa Rosa, California 95403, USA
Telephone: (USA 001) 707 579 4452
www.schulzmuseum.org

'Try not to have a good time ... this is supposed to be educational.'
Sally, Peanuts museum-visiting cartoon, 7 May 1971

Good Grief! A Peanuts Museum? What next? Like the creator of the Peanuts comic strip, Charles M. Schulz, his eponymous museum is full of charming quirks. This museum embraces the Snoopy-inspired work of avant-garde artists, as well as genuine historical Snoopyabilia.

Schulz's timeless comic strip had its first outing in October 1950. Fifty years later, his cast of characters were household names in 75 countries.

The modest artist himself was at first unsure about the idea of a museum. 'Sparky', as he was known to family and friends, didn't see himself as a museum piece. But as the Peanuts 50th anniversary approached, the idea gathered momentum. Sadly, Sparky did not live to see the museum open in 2002. He died of cancer in February 2000, much mourned by his millions of fans.

The museum concept came from the artist's wife Jean, and friends. It was built not far from the place where Schulz lived and worked, a stone's throw from the Warm Puppy Café where he ate breakfast, overlooking the ice rink where he played hockey.

The core of the museum's collection is, of course, the original cartoon strips. Over 7,000 have been preserved here, as well as pages of doodles saved from the wastepaper basket by his secretary, who carefully ironed them.

On the second floor is a recreation of 'Sparky's Studio' at One Snoopy Place in Santa Rosa. Behind a low screen, the visitor sees the drawing board that the artist used most of his working life, his desk and armchair. The walls are covered with notes and cards. In an adjoining gallery, glass cases contain the artist's personal belongings, such as his boyhood baseball gloves, army sketchbook, family photos and a scrapbook of comics published before Peanuts made him the world's most beloved cartoonist.

Snoopy and Charlie Brown, so cemented in the public imagination, did not spring forth fully formed. They evolved. And the 'archaeology' of Peanuts – the equivalent of ancient cave paintings in this impatient modern world – can be seen in a wall that has been carefully removed from a house in Colorado Springs where Schulz lived in 1951. The colourful nursery collage had long been painted over. But later owners Polly and Stanley Travnicek, hearing rumours of their existence, painstakingly uncovered the pictures with Red Devil Sandy Liquid. They show a Snoopy who still walked on four paws instead of upright, and Charlie Brown jumping over a candlestick. When the couple heard about the new museum, they decided to donate the wall.

The journey of rediscovery continues with *Morphing Snoopy*, a vast wood sculpture created by the Japanese artist Yoshiteru Otani. *Morphing Snoopy* consists of 43 separate layers that reveal the evolving character of Snoopy, beginning with Spike, Schulz's childhood pet, the inspiration for the world's most recognisable black-and-white beagle. Another Otani work is a 3,500-piece tile mural, showing Charlie Brown's heartbreaking attempts to kick a ball.

In the museum's garden, Lea Goode-Harris has created a labyrinth in the shape of Snoopy's head. Another special exhibit is Christo's *Wrapped Snoopy House*. The French artists Christo and Jeanne-Claude created a sensation in the 1970s by 'wrapping' vast monuments like the Pont Neuf in Paris in fabric. Schulz paid tribute to their work in a 1978 comic strip: Snoopy's iconic doghouse swaddled in fabric 'à-la-Christo'. The compliment was returned 25 years later, when Christo himself created a real, life-size *Wrapped Snoopy House* for the museum.

Of course, fans can get close to their master by investing in the merchandise in the museum store, but easily the most poignant and intimate experience to be had here is Jean Schulz's moving, simple video, describing her husband's life and the creation of this museum. The video can be viewed on the website.

THE DALÍ THEATRE-MUSEUM

Plaça de Gala i Salvador Dalí 5, 17600 Figueres, Girona, Spain
Telephone: (Spain 0034) 972 677500 / 972 677509
www.salvador-dali.org

'Where, if not in my own town, should the most extravagant and solid of my work endure, where if not here?'

Salvador Dalí

Figueres, near the Spanish–French border, was the birthplace of the famous surrealist artist (1904–89). The town's ruined theatre was converted into a highly theatrical museum for him in 1974. Dalí himself embellished the façade (topped by a geodesic dome in a nest of dinosaur-sized white eggs). He also designed the interiors and, of course, provided the 4,000 extraordinary exhibits.

Don't expect chronologies, explanations or a logical path through this relentlessly eccentric edifice. This is a museum of surrealism, remember. And one created by surrealism's greatest protagonist, partly as a tribute to himself, but also in homage to his wife and muse Gala.

This is museum as autobiography – the couple's faces and bodies figure everywhere, as do references to the dynamics of their relationship. Crutches, for example, because Dalí always said that he needed Gala to lean on. In the Palace of the Wind room, a ceiling fresco shows the couples' departing feet as they fly up to heaven. There's his *Portrait of Gala with Two Lamb Chops In Equilibrium upon Her Shoulder* from circa 1934, and from 1978 a stereoscopic work, *Dalí Lifting the Skin of the*

Mediterranean Sea to Show Gala the Birth of Venus. In the museum's vine-clad central courtyard there's a 1978 installation named *Car-naval*. Dalí's own 1941 Cadillac has a coin-op mechanism to make it rain inside the car. Beside that, atop a tower of car tyres, is Gala's little boat, dripping blue tears made of condoms.

Bread, a key Dalí symbol, features strongly in the museum as decoration and art. When Dalí first got off the plane in the United States, he insisted on wearing a loaf of bread on his head.

Dalí was fascinated with Mae West. His witty iconoclasm and her free spirit were natural partners. There's a whole room dedicated to her here, including her face represented as an apartment. His famous 'lips' sofa is based on the lush mouth of the star known for her salacious quips.

Not all the paintings in the museum are originals, for Dalí regarded himself as a 'whore' of art and often sold his original work to the highest bidder. But there's a core of important real work, including *Port Alguer* (1923); *The Spectre of Sex Appeal* (1934); *Soft Self-Portrait with Fried Bacon* (1941); *Napoleon's Nose Transformed into a Pregnant Woman, Strolling Her Shadow with Melancholic amongst Original Ruins* (1945); *The Basket of Bread* (1945); and *Atomic Leda* (1949).

The museum shows Dalí's skills as an irrepressible technical innovator. He used holograms to create 360° views, and layers and mirrors to make 3D art, as in his *Gala Nude Watching the Sea which, at a Distance of 20 Metres, Turns Into the Portrait of Abraham Lincoln* (1975). His portrait of Beethoven was done in squid ink applied with a shoe during a stormy night. He chose to depict Jesus with candle smoke and an eraser.

A separate exhibit shows the surrealist jewellery designed by Dalí in gold and precious stones between 1949 and 1970.

Finally, visitors can pay homage to the master at the artist's surprisingly simple stone crypt, situated in the heart of the museum: a fitting final resting place, for the museum itself is undoubtedly the world's largest surrealist work of art.

SCHIMPFF'S CONFECTIONERY MUSEUM

347 Spring Street, Jeffersonville, Indiana 47130, USA
Telephone: (USA 001) 812 283 8367
www.schimpffs.com

*'Many visitors come with their children and grandchildren in tow,
sharing stories and making connections with the past.'*
Jill Schimpff, curator

Remember those Horehound Drops, the Hard Fish Candy and, of course, the Cinnamon Red Hots? What about the caramel-covered marshmallow Modjeskas? No? But don't you wish you did?

All are famous 'signature' sweets manufactured by Schimpff's Confectionery, an Indiana institution since 1891, and still a successful family business, now in its fourth generation and still rustling up the same sweet somethings in the same historic premises in Jeffersonville's old town centre.

Schimpff's founder, Gustav Schimpff Sr, was just a boy when he left Germany in the 1840s. His mother, Magdalene, was widowed while pregnant with her eighth child. Despite having no relatives in America, the brave woman decided to emigrate, choosing an area where German-speakers were living in large numbers. Her young son Gustav, with no previous experience in the trade, set up the business that eventually became Schimpff's Confectionery. Schimpff's is, in fact, the oldest retail business in town, and has survived the Depression, deaths in the family and serious flooding, remaining open for all but one of the last 116 years.

In the same place there's also a retail store and restaurant complete with a functioning 1950s soda fountain and glass jars of candy on shelves stacked right up to the ceiling. In 2001 the family acquired the building next door and opened a 'living museum' dedicated to the American candy industry.

In the 'Candy Kitchen' the visitors can witness the turn-of-the-century techniques in sweet-making. The 550-square-metre (1,800-square-foot) Candy Museum shows a collection of several thousand candy tins and wrappers, as well as moulds, posters, signs and antique machinery. These were collected in a nationwide pilgrimage by Jill and Warren Schimpff, who continue with their quest, refreshing their holdings constantly. This is a museum in sensurround – while browsing the colourful shelves, the scents of melted chocolate and boiling sugar from the working machines swirl around the visitor.

Guided tours are offered by appointment and you can hear stories of many forgotten stars of confectionery history. The hand-dipped Modjeskas, by the way, were named after a famous Polish actress who debuted Henrik Ibsen's *A Doll's House* in Louisville in 1883.

Schimpff's is still making its Cinnamon Red Hots and other hard candies from recipes in the book written by their founder Gustav Schimpff and his son, Gustav Jr. Like their forebears, Jill and Warren Schimpff live 'above the shop' and talk, breathe and live candy. They had been living in California when the last of the previous generation died out. Warren had been a closet candy-maker in his garage, and when the opportunity beckoned, the couple felt 'called' to take over a business that now rules their lives.

This is one museum visit where the visitor will be pleased to take away free samples, or to buy the merchandise (five pounds of candy that cost 33 cents in 1891 now fetch $30). Don't miss the white chocolate rats with red eyes, mysteriously popular for Valentine's Day in Jeffersonville. Jill Schimpff recounts: 'One burly truck driver got his wife a three-pound heart box of chocolates with a white rat carefully positioned in the centre. He took out the chocolate next to the rat's mouth and then bit off a piece before replacing it in the box! Let's hope the wife had a good sense of humour, too!' The white chocolate rats have also been delivered along with divorce papers.

Traditional treats mix with modern innovations. You can, for example, order a 'Shrek Sundae' these days.

So many children still press their noses against Schimpff's plate-glass windows that the staff have thoughtfully provided a step and rails to make the candy voyeurism safer.

THE MORPETH CHANTRY BAGPIPE MUSEUM

Bridge Street, Morpeth, Northumberland NE61 1PJ, England
Telephone: (UK 0044) (0)1670 500717
www.bagpipemuseum.org.uk

'Bagpipes are not just a lot of hot air, best heard three glens away.'
Anne Moore, curator

This award-winning museum is housed in a 13th-century structure that has served as a religious building, a grammar school, a mineral water factory and a ladies' lavatory. It was rescued from this spiral of misfortune in the 1980s and now houses a craft centre and the local tourist information office as well as its principal attraction – the most comprehensive collection of bagpipes on display in the world. The major part of the display was bequeathed to the Society of Antiquaries of Newcastle upon Tyne by the great collector and archivist of bagpipes, William Alfred Cocks.

The first thing you learn at this stylish museum is that bagpipes are not just a Scottish phenomenon. Nor are they solely intended to wake up the neighbours or terrify the enemy in war. Pipes are among the most ancient of musical instruments. They've been played in Great Britain for at least 800 years. They are still regularly played in Northumberland, Scotland, Ireland, all over Europe, and in Asia and North Africa. Each area has its own version, and examples, photographs and recordings of them have been gathered together at Morpeth Chantry.

There's the *bombarde* and *biniou* from Brittany, the French *musette de cour*, the *gaita* from Spain, the Bohemian *dudy*, the *zampogna* from Italy and the *kava gaida* from Bulgaria – to mention but a few. In Germany, the bagpipe rejoices in the name *Dudelsack*.

The museum explains the physics of bagpipe sound. Most bagpipes consist of a bag to store air and at least three tubes – the recorder-like chanter, which provides the melody, the drones for harmony, and the mouthpiece for blowing in air. Some models have bellows that are pumped by the player's arm.

Within that configuration, there's a world of variation, according to whether you're playing the Highland bagpipes (big and loud and best for outdoors); the Northumbrian small pipes (smaller, sweeter, quieter and good indoors); Border or half-long pipes; the Irish Union or Uilleann pipes; Greek shepherd's pipes; or the Sardinian *launeddas*. And a skilful piper can coax any kind of music from his instrument – baroque, jazz and even pop.

Since the 16th century, the bagpipes have been very much an instrument of the people, though rusticating aristocrats were known to affect a little bagpipe-playing in the 1800s. A notorious figure in the world of bagpipes was James Allan – deserter, serial marrier, horse-thief and friend of royalty. His bagpipes are in the museum. The House of Percy was the only noble family in England to employ a piper as a family retainer. Two hundred years later, the post still exists.

A sophisticated infrared sound system allows the visitor to listen to the sounds of different bagpipes through headphones while looking at the actual instrument that produces it. Each instrument is displayed in its actual playing position. Other exhibits include historical scores of bagpipe music and the stories of famous and infamous pipers.

If you want a real bagpipe treat, visit the museum on a Saturday afternoon when you may catch the Northumbrian Pipers' Society playing. This group has been meeting since 1928. The museum also runs classes, undertaking to have a complete novice play a recognisable tune after just one day of tuition.

There's a Museum of Piping in Glasgow, Scotland, too: www.thepipingcentre.co.uk.

THE MUSTARD MUSEUM

100 West Main Street, Mount Horeb, Wisconsin 53572, USA
Telephone: (USA 001) 608 437 3986
www.mustardweb.com

'Mustard is like a canvas, allowing the creation of great works of culinary art.'   Barry Levenson, founder

To understand the privileged position of mustard in the hearts of Americans, it's important to realise that they eat *20 billion hot dogs a year*, and that most of the pink sausages in those soft white buns are slathered with the vivid yellow condiment.

Given this statistic, it's not surprising that a museum has been dedicated to mustard. The curator, Barry Levenson, was called to the cause in the early hours of 28 October 1986, when his beloved Boston Red Sox lost the baseball World Series. The mortified fan wandered around an all-night grocery, looking for edible consolation. He found mustard – and an epiphany. Americans love mustard, it came to Barry Levenson, then and there. Therefore Americans would come in droves to a mustard museum.

And they have. Levenson, formerly a Wisconsin Assistant Attorney-General, has left the day job long behind him and now works exclusively on his mustard collection and his mustard retail business. Not to mention his role as dean of students at Poupon U, the official mustard college. The college band's songbook includes such condimentally correct classics as 'Roll Out the Mustard!', 'Have Your Seen the Mustard Man?' and 'Yellow

Mustard Jar'. Levenson also finds time to author books such as *Habeas Codfish: Reflections on Food and the Law*.

Barry Levenson's Mustard Museum is the world's largest collection of mustard bottles, boxes, tubes, advertising and memorabilia. The doors opened in 1992, with just 1,000 mustards. The collection has now risen to 4,700 and includes mustards from 50 American states and 60 countries around the world.

The Tasting Table allows visitors to sample all kinds of mustards, including some flavoured with Roquefort cheese, tequila, cranberry or wasabi lime. Don't miss the special Noyo Reserve Merlot'n'Chocolate Mustard. The visitor can compare the historic British Colman's mustard with the elegant pale yellow product from Dijon, France.

An international history of mustard is explained in a video in the Mustard Piece Theatre. Among other things to learn: mustard's violent colour belies a gentle interior. The key ingredient, mustard flour, contains only 4.3 calories per gram. The bright colour comes from the spice turmeric. It's the additional spices that fire up the burning taste (and the label poetry) of mustards such as Dave's Hurtin' Habañero and Smack My Ass and Call me Sally Hot Sauce (both available in a gift box known as 'Love Hurts'). The heat gets turned up in another gift box known as 'Burning Desires'. This includes Cherchies Hold on Hannah! Hot Mustard, Ass Kickin' Chili Fixins and Dave's Burning Nuts.

A good time to visit the Mustard Museum is National Mustard Day, the first Saturday in August. On that occasion, the Mustard gang paints the town yellow with mustard games and mustard music. Free hot dogs are available for all, and for afters there's refreshing mustard ice cream.

The museum's gift shop publishes 'America's Steamiest Gourmet Catalogue', full of legendary mustard brands like Hit and Run, with flavours that range from 'Wickedly Hot' horseradish and 'Sinus-Clearing' yellow horseradish to 'Excruciatingly Painful' brown horseradish. Or there's Killer Bee Radical Raspberry Honey Mustard and local product Wisconsin Wilderness Cranberry Mustard, or exotic Beaver Russian Mustard and even spiritual Benedictine Sisters Monastery Mustard in Heavenly Honey flavour.

'Occasion' mustards are also available: Congratulations on Your Retirement Aioli Garlic Mustard and Merry Christmas Reindeer Beer Mustard.

British mustard enthusiasts can visit the Colman's Mustard Shop and Museum in Norwich, Norfolk. There are also mustard museums in Doesburg, the Netherlands (Boekholtstraat 22, Doesburg, 6984 CW), and Dijon, France (48 quai Nicolas Rolin, Dijon 21000).

THE CAT MUSEUM

Kuching North City Hall Building, Bukit Siol,
Jalan Semariang, Petra Jaya,
Kuching, Sarawak (Borneo), Malaysia
Telephone: (Malaysia 0060) (0)82 446688 extension 805
www.dbku.gov.my/catmuseum.htm

*'Women's hearts belong to the Cat. For women the Cat is serving
as an unattainable ideal of beauty and grace. It is also an incarnation of independence and freedom – unlimited freedom – which
makes it twice as attractive for any woman.'*

Andrei Abramov, director of the Moscow Cat Museum

Perched high on a hill in Kuching, capital of the east Malaysian state of Sarawak, this large and imposing museum
contains over 2,000 cat artefacts from around the world.

The collection was originally housed in the National
Museum of Kuala Lumpur, but was transferred to Kuching in
1988, an appropriate move, given that 'Kuching' translates into
'cat' in Malay.

This name, however, is said to have arisen out of a mis-
understanding. When the Englishman Sir James Brooke arrived
in 1841 to become the first white rajah of Sarawak, he pointed
in the direction of his new capital and asked its name. His trans-
lator thought he was pointing at a small feral cat crouching in
the undergrowth, and answered 'kuching'. The name stuck, and
these days statues of cats can be found all around the town.

The museum itself is in the district of Petra Jaya, up a very
steep hill. The Malaysian Ministry of Tourism warns: 'By car, you

will need to ensure that your brake is in good condition due to its hilltop location.'

Among the highlights: the only known stuffed specimen of the rarest cat in the world, *Felis badia*, from the rainforests of Borneo. Golden brown and chestnut in colour, it has a white patch on the underside of the tail to its tip. The museum's specimen is mounted without internal bones, the curators explain, 'and therefore does not look perfect'.

Other local cats are featured too. And what magnificent beasts they are! The rare *harimau dahan*, largest of all Bornean cats, is striped in orange like a tiger. Arboreal, it hunts monkeys. *Felis bengalensis*, the beauty queen of cats, with its black spots on a tawny yellow coat, is a prestigious breed in the West, and dines only on the most expensive brands of cat food. In Sarawak the Bengal cat lives wild, is usually nocturnal, and feeds on small mammals and birds including domestic chickens.

The history of the domestic cat is recounted in tableaux, followed by a section on famous cat-lovers and their cats, including Charles Dickens, Winston Churchill and Theodore Roosevelt. Less famous cat-lovers are cited for outstanding feline devotion – for example, there's a lady who had her deceased pet cremated, then mixed the ashes with tattoo ink and had the image of the cat tattooed on her leg.

There's also a section on the influence of cats on human music-making, not just the eponymous musical from Messrs Eliot and Lloyd-Webber, but songs dating back to the 19th century, such as 'The Cat Came Back' and the 1921 jazz classic 'Kitten on the Keys'.

Popular culture is not neglected – there are cat models on a catwalk, a dangling statue of Catwoman, Black Cat cigarettes, Garfield, Tom and Jerry and Felix the Cat, who paces back and forth on the website.

The museum is also a research centre for scholars wishing to delve into historical, social and legendary cat matters. The museum describes itself as 'a meeting place for all researchers and cat-lovers from all over the world'.

There's a rival establishment in Moscow these days, a travelling museum of art and artefacts. The elaborate website (www.moscowcatmuseum.com) explains the history and philosophy of the collection, with a great emphasis on the bond between women and cats. Also posted are photos of the pulchritudinous winners of the Woman and Cat beauty contest since 1994.

THE MUSEUM OF THE AMERICAN PRINTING HOUSE FOR THE BLIND

1839 Frankfort Avenue, Louisville, Kentucky 40206, USA
Telephone: (USA 001) 859 895 2405
www.aph.org/museum

'Museums and art stores are also sources of pleasure and inspiration. Doubtless it will seem strange to many that the hand unaided by sight can feel action, sentiment, beauty in the cold marble; and yet it is true that I derive genuine pleasure from touching great works of art. As my fingertips trace line and curve, they discover the thought and emotion which the artist has portrayed.'

Helen Keller, *The Story of My Life*, chapter XXII, 1903

Helen Keller thought that blind people derived even more joy from sculpture than sighted ones. Conversely, there's a huge reward for sighted people who care to cross the line, and experiment with experiencing life as a blind person. This is something they can do at the Museum of the American Printing House for the Blind.

'Kids love it, although they're very dubious when they first arrive. Blindness is pretty frightening for both kids and adults', explains Micheal A. Hudson, director. 'We try to overcome that fear by showing people through time who have struggled to overcome obstacles to literacy and learning.'

This museum is probably the only one in the world that celebrates literacy for the blind. As such, it's a wonderfully tactile place, and all visitors, sighted or not, are encouraged to handle as many of the exhibits as possible. Visitors can create their own names in Braille, use an abacus, feel an outline of the world on a raised map. A computer game tests visitors' mental arithmetic skills on problems from a book printed at the American Printing House for the Blind in 1873.

It's a sobering thought that schools for blind children were not opened in America until the 1830s. Even then, teachers were obliged to make their own equipment, or import embossed books from Europe. So it was a revolutionary step forward when the American Printing House for the Blind was set up in 1858, the brainchild of Dempsey Sherrod, a blind man from Mississippi. The very first book printed by the press was *Fables and Tales for Children* – in an embossed letter type, many years before the standardisation of Braille. The press printed its first Braille publication in 1892. Today it's the world's largest manufacturer of books and aids for the blind.

As early as 1936, the company set up a recording studio for talking books, and it produced the first human-voice encyclopaedia in 1981. In the meantime it was pioneering the production of writing and calculating aids for the blind – the New Hall Braille Writer in 1940 and the Cranmer Abacus in 1963.

The museum opened in 1994, and was renamed in 1999 in honour of two benefactors, the Marie and Eugene Callahan Museum of the American Printing House for the Blind.

Artefacts include historical tactile books, maps, educational aids, mechanical writers, historical Braille production machinery, phonographic recording equipment and players, photographs and illustrations. The exhibits are, of course, accessible to all, with audio-phones, Braille labels, and touchable exhibits for blind visitors.

One of the oldest and most unusual exhibits is the McElroy Point Writing Machine from 1888. The smallest writer in the collection is a Minerva Pocket Braillewriter, made in Germany about 1900, which measures 15 x 12.5 x 6 centimetres (6" x 5" x 2.5"). There are also Braille writing slates, music-reading equipment and maps of the world for blind people to travel round with their fingertips.

Other inspiring exhibits explain the life and work of Louis Braille, and that of Helen Keller, America's most famous example of a blind person who succeeded against all odds.

THE ROCK'N'ROLL HALL OF SHAME

Online at www.fadetoblack.com/hallofshame

'Most people get into bands for three very simple rock and roll reasons: to get laid, to get fame, and to get rich.'   Bob Geldof

This all-singing site reveals what some Hollywood legends would rather forget: their recording careers. Here you can hear clips of Telly Savalas droning 'You've Lost That Loving Feeling', Mae West sounding remarkably like Margaret Thatcher in 'Day Tripper' and Andy Griffith burning down 'The House of the Rising Sun'.

The site muses on what motivates people who plainly cannot sing to record this fact on vinyl. 'Is it', they ask, 'the mandatory narcissistic obsession that comes with being a star? Is it the constant exposure to drugs and alcohol? Is it the close proximity of greasy executives and slimy producers who are out to exploit anyone and everyone to make a buck?'

All of the above, it seems.

Yoko Ono switches between yodelling, shrieking and vibrato in her recording of 'John, John'. 'Little' Joe Pesci battles through 'Got to Get You Into My Life'. Leonard Nimoy takes all the pride out of 'Proud Mary'. ('Before you judge, remember, Vulcans had no emotions. None.')

Pat Boone is honoured with thirteen entries, including 'Stairway to Heaven', 'Paradise City' and 'You've Got Another Thing Comin''. The site comments: 'What do you get when you cross a gospel singer your parents liked with the guitar-driven hard rock songs you like? Music you can both agree is God awful.'

Some of the singers surely had their tongues in their cheeks when they recorded these monsterpieces. Phyllis Diller, for example, warbles 'I Can't Get No Satisfaction' in a way that makes clear she's never going to get any.

Even great singers make mistakes, like Bing Crosby's ill-advised recording of 'Hey Jude'. His famously subtle phrasing is just too subtle for this song.

The Rock'n'Roll Hall of Shame is part of the Fade to Black comedy website. The 'mother-ship' is well worth a visit. There are interviews with Emo Philips, Harry Shearer and Bill Hicks. There's also a blackly humorous sequence of correspondence with companies like Kimberly-Clark and Colgate Palmolive in which a 'child' tries to give away his pet rabbit for animal testing. Fade to Black also publishes online the FBI file on the comedian Lenny Bruce. And there's a visitor poll on the Top Ten Celebrities Most Likely to Die.

Glenn Gould once observed that a record is a concert without halls, and a museum whose curator is the owner. For more excruciating music clips curated with witty commentary, visit Frank's Vinyl Museum, 'the Internet Home of Weird Records', at http://franklarosa.com/vinyl. Telly's there, and Donny and Marie, but also vintage television jingles like the Banana Splits' lobotomising 'Tra-la-la' song. And don't miss 'Gracias Por La Musica', Abba singing their hits in Spanish. 'Reina Danzante' doesn't sound quite the same as 'Dancing Queen'.

THE BUFFALO BILL MUSEUM AND GRAVE

Lookout Mountain, 987 Lookout Mountain Road,
Golden, Colorado 80401, USA
Telephone: (USA 001) 303 526 0744
www.buffalobill.org

'Some people in Wyoming insist that Buffalo Bill wished to be buried in their state. But according to Buffalo Bill's widow, his priest, his daughter, his sisters and his foster son, he asked to be buried on Lookout Mountain in Colorado. The preponderance of evidence clearly supports his present resting place. It seems that some folks manage to live in two states: Wyoming and denial.'

Steve Friesen, director

According to his widow Louisa, Cody chose this spot for its incomparable view.

His grave is appropriately rugged and macho. Built of rough-hewn stones, the tombstone nestles amid the fragrant ponderosa pines and looks out on the dramatic high peaks that formed the backdrop to what was surely the ultimate Wild West lifestyle.

Visitors often throw coins onto the grave. Director Steve Friesen explains: 'In the 1920s a group of Lakota Sioux warriors visited and placed Indian head/buffalo nickels on the grave in tribute to Buffalo Bill ... People continue to throw money on the grave, probably thinking it might give them luck, just like when they throw money in a wishing well. There is also a story of single women throwing bobby pins on the grave in hopes it will help them get married.'

Close by Buffalo Bill's grave is the museum that honours his life – with such gusto that one of its regular annual events is a rollicking Buffalo Bill's birthday party on the last Sunday of each February (including the keenly contested Buffalo chip-tossing contest). Some years the museum presents a re-enactment of Cody's burial, complete with a grieving widow and a cavalry salute.

Born in 1846, William F. Cody was a red-blooded hero of American folk history. He did it all: Cody was a gold miner, a wagon-train driver, a trapper, a Civil War soldier, a Pony Express rider and an army frontier scout. He earned his nickname 'Buffalo Bill' for his prowess in hunting down the massive beasts to feed America's railroad workers.

In 1883 Cody set up the show known as Buffalo Bill's Wild West, starring himself as himself. For 30 years the educational frontier spectacular toured America, with horse parades, displays of sharp-shooting and re-enactments of stage-coach ambushes and Custer's Last Stand. Among Cody's cast were real Indians, including Sitting Bull; also Annie Oakley and Calamity Jane. Press coverage meant that Cody was for a time the owner of the best-known American face in the world. He was a featured attraction at Queen Victoria's Golden Jubilee.

Despite his image as the all-American tough guy, Cody was at heart a reformer. He believed that women should have the vote, and spoke out against mistreatment of the Indians. He also campaigned against reckless recreational hunting.

The Buffalo Bill Memorial Museum was founded in 1921, four years after Cody's death. The founder was the great man's foster son Johnny Baker, who had worked as a marksman with the Wild West shows. Baker was uniquely placed to collect original artefacts from Cody's life. On display in the museum the visitor can see a lock of Buffalo Bill's hair; his silver-mounted saddle; the buckskins he sported in the Wild West show; the outfit he wore at his final public performance on 11 November 1916; and the last cartridge he ever fired from a gun. Other exhibits include historical timelines of Buffalo Bill's life and an exhibit on his relationship with the Indians.

The museum also has a temporary exhibit area for changing thematic displays, such as 'The Reel West: Cliché and Character at the Saturday Matinee'.

The original museum was set up in a large spruce log cabin which was named Pahaska Tepee. Pahaska (Long Hair) was the name the Sioux Indians bestowed on Buffalo Bill. The city of Denver took over the museum in 1957 and built a modern facility for the historical artefacts in 1979. The Tepee now serves as the café (where you can dine on Buffalo Burgers and Buffalo Chilli) and an extensive gift shop, stocked with Americana and Wild West memorabilia.

Other modern facilities include a children's activity area where visitors can put on cowboy clothing and sit on a horse for photographs.

THE TRUFFLE MUSEUM

Piazza Gramsci 1, 53020 San Giovanni d'Asso, Siena, Italy
Telephone: (Italy 0039) 0577 803268 / 340 645 2336 (mobile)
www.museodeltartufo.it

'Whosoever says truffle, utters a grand word, which awakens erotic and gastronomic ideas …'

Jean-Anthelme Brillat-Savarin

Allow yourself to be blindfolded, and enter the 'Odor-ama'. See how many different truffles you can sniff before the musky funk of the world's most expensive and ugliest fungus wafts you into a stupor.

Truffles are reputed to be potent aphrodisiacs. The science is in the smell, which has a proven tranquillising effect on the human spirit. A relaxed mood generally puts people in the mood for love.

The Romans first recognised the aphrodisiac qualities of the truffle. Plutarch claimed that truffles were born when lightning struck damp earth. So mysterious and powerful was the globular tuber that it was sometimes considered as an animal rather than a plant. Its sulphurous fumes gave rise to a superstition that the truffle was the food of the devil, or at least witches. The only things everyone agreed on: it was rare, and delicious, and correspondingly expensive – 'the garlic of the rich'.

Succeeding generations of Italians have mined these 'white diamonds' assiduously, none more so than the villagers of San Giovanni d'Asso, in truffle-rich Tuscany. In 2004 the village opened its own museum inside a gruff medieval castle. Two hundred and fifty square metres (2,700 square feet) of display space are divided into four main 'nuclei' curated with the help of chefs, pharmacists and botanists.

Visitors learn about the history and legends of truffles, experience the sensations of a truffle hunt in the 'Odor-ama' and then take a journey right to the centre of the truffle, literally walking inside a giant model of the fungus. Another section is devoted to the culinary history of truffles. Displays show the history of truffle-hunting in Italy, and modern techniques for finding the precious boles. There's a truffle map of Italy and videos of truffle-hunting, truffle chefs and truffle-eaters.

Truffles, the visitor learns, like to nestle in the roots of certain tree species, particularly oaks. In Italy, dogs are preferred to pigs for truffle-hunting – apparently they are less likely to devour the goodies. Truffle dogs change hands for enormous sums, and in the cut-throat world of truffling, dogs have been nobbled or even poisoned.

The prizes are rich indeed. White truffles, rarer and costlier, are sold at auction in Italy. A truffle weighing 1.2 kilograms (2.6 pounds) can fetch £64,000 ($112,000), with bidders calling in their offers via satellite from Hong Kong and New York. There are even websites that function as a kind of truffle stock exchange: www.albatartufi.com for white truffles, and www.acqualegna. info for the black truffle.

There are tales of truffle tragedy too. A huge truffle, sold for £30,000 ($52,000) in 2004, rotted away and died before the winning bidder, a London restaurant, could make use of it. The monster tuber was taken back to Italy for a gala funeral and interment in the ground of its home town of San Miniato. A solemn service was held for the defunct truffle, which was draped in blue velvet and accompanied to its grave by a drummer.

The truffle has been a source of political gain and creative inspiration as well as a delicacy to excite the animal appetites. The museum explains that Count Camillo Benso di Cavour used the truffle as a diplomatic tool. Rossini claimed that the truffle was the 'Mozart of Mushrooms' and Lord Byron (the Italians' favourite Englishman) kept a truffle on his desk, thinking that the perfume would enhance his creativity.

The museum's website, in Italian, gives recipes for polenta, risotto and pasta with truffles, not to mention *crostini* and *fagottini* ...

THE NATIONAL MUSEUM OF
FUNERAL HISTORY

415 Barren Springs Drive, Houston, Texas 77090, USA
Telephone: (USA 001) 281 876 3063
www.nmfh.org

'Any day above the ground is a good one.'

That's the catchphrase for the merchandise sold at what turns out to be a very upbeat take on a gloomy subject. This enormous museum opened in 1992. At 1,860 square metres (20,000 square feet), it is without doubt the largest museum in the world devoted to the arts of death.

Among thousands of objects, lovingly arranged, are beautiful glass caskets, fairytale glass funeral coaches, elegant motorised hearses from the 1920s and mementoes of the funerals of the famous, including J.F. Kennedy, Elvis Presley, Judy Garland and John Wayne. There's a replica of Abraham Lincoln's decorated coffin and a photograph of the president inside it. King Tutankhamen's gilded coffin is also reproduced in detail and to size.

A professional guide conducts one-hour tours of the exhibition, explaining and answering questions. Three films explain the changing traditions and techniques of burial around the world.

Among more recent highlights are twelve carved and painted Ghanaian 'fantasy coffins', in the shapes of a Mercedes Benz, a leopard, a chicken, a bull, a shallot, a crab, an eagle, a fish, a lobster, a Yamaha outboard motor, a KLM aeroplane and a fishing canoe.

President J. F. Kennedy's Eternal Flame is on permanent loan to the museum. Originally commissioned in 1963, the mechanism has been upgraded with new technology that is explained in the exhibit.

And not to be missed is the black Toyota truck with a pagoda roof. It's equipped with speakers to play sombre music at Japanese funerals. There's also a graceful 19th-century Mohr & Birdboro funeral sled and a recreation of a 1920s embalming studio.

A diorama illustrates battlefield embalming conducted during the Civil War by the famous Dr Holmes, who charged $7 for an enlisted man and $13 for an officer.

The museum is run as a charitable institution and raises funds with its National Museum of Funeral History annual Golf Classic held at the Kingwood Country Club, the filming location of the movie *Tin Cup*.

The gift shop sells baseball caps, T-shirts and coffee mugs branded with the catchphrase. And golf balls, of course. It also offers model hearses and videos such as *The Curse of King Tut* and *The St Valentine's Day Massacre*.

The museum's website publishes a wish list of items that are still being sought to perfect the collection. In case anyone is clearing out the attic, these are the things they are looking for: undertaking signs from the 1800s; mourning clothing; jewellery and photographs; church trucks; Civil War memorabilia; and newspaper cuttings about American presidential funerals and funerals of the famous.

The Undertakers' Museum in Vienna, Austria, is worth a visit. Housed in the Municipal Undertaking Institute at Goldegasse 19, it displays caskets, mourning clothes, death masks, coffins and urns; funeral vehicles; shrouds; death notices, including those of Beethoven and Strauss; and invitations to the funeral of the Emperor Franz Josef. It shows how corpses were once dressed up and propped up on a chair for one last photograph. There's also an ingenious device to stop accidental burial of people who are still alive: a bell was attached to a rope within the coffin, allowing the occupant to raise the alarm if he should wake up.

Real enthusiasts might also want to take a look at the Museum of Sepulchral Culture in Kassel, Germany, and the Hearse Museum in Barcelona, Spain.

THE SWISS MUSEUM OF GAMES

Au Château de La Tour-de-Peilz, CH-1814, Switzerland
Telephone: (Switzerland 0041) (0)21 977 2300
www.museedujeu.com (in French)

'A stereotyped but unconscious despair is concealed even under what are called the games and amusements of mankind.'

Henry David Thoreau

Although we humans like to style ourselves *Homo sapiens*, wise man, a more accurate title might be *Homo ludens* – games-playing man.

Games-playing is universal to mankind, to both genders, to all ages and all races, to the intellectual and the illiterate, to the poor and the rich.

And games are never just games. They should be taken seriously, both as rehearsals for life and a way of hiding from life. Eric Berne, author of *Games People Play* (1964), suggested that games were an important way of controlling our emotional lives, being a compromise between intimacy and keeping intimacy at bay.

No one, it seems, takes their games more seriously than the Swiss. In 1984, far-sighted Swiss academics started collecting all kinds of games, dividing them with, well, *Swiss precision* into the different aspects of game-playing. These, it emerges, are Pleasure, Freedom, Fiction, Rules, Fighting, Gratuitousness and Uncertainty.

(Are you still having fun?)

The good news is that the Swiss Museum of Games now offers the public a chance to see beautiful and fascinating games and toys from throughout the ages and from all over the world – and that this is one museum where playing with the exhibits is part of the visit. Here children and adults have proper play-corners in which to exercise their strategic, psychological, analytical and manual skills.

This very serious playhouse is set inside a lovely little 13th-century chateau, like an overgrown toy model of a castle, complete with turrets and shutters, on the edge of a picturesque Swiss lake. The chateau was once the defensive stronghold for the Counts of Savoy. In 1979, after literally going through the wars (too numerous to mention), it became the property of the commune of the Tour-de-Peilz and was opened to the public. The 550-square-metre (6,000-square-foot) Museum of Games was inaugurated in 1987.

There are over 250 games on display, including the familiar and the unusual, from the sophisticated devices of the casino to the humble jigsaw. The museum's holdings start with games from Ancient Egypt dating back to the third millennium BC. There's a grinning *bilboquet* from 1900 – a wooden clown with a ruff and a pointy hat to throw on his head, all kinds of board games from French 'goose' to the intricate Indian *mancala* and *pachisi*, the African *awele* and the Korean *nyout*. There are highly decorative collections of playing cards and chess pieces from around the world. Many of the vividly painted toys show the distressed patina of loving use.

'Games are much more than a pastime, they are a real cultural acquisition', says the museum's Rita Schyrr. 'Wherever people come from, whatever their tradition, they unite in play – by communicating spontaneously and naturally.'

A specialised library is available to researchers. But for ordinary games-players, the museum's shop stocks a tasteful selection of toys, and the Domino Café sets out its tables and chairs in the picturesque courtyard of the chateau.

THE DAKOTA DINOSAUR MUSEUM

200 East Museum Drive, Dickinson,
North Dakota 58601, USA
Telephone: (USA 001) 701 225 3466
www.dakotadino.com

'Almost all children love dinosaurs and are not afraid of even the biggest animals. Once in a while a child might be initially afraid if they have previously been to a robotic dinosaur display where the dinosaurs showed some movement and they thought they were alive. But the fear passes and they are soon off to see the dinosaurs while holding their parent's hand.'

Larry League, curator

Most people get the dino bug as kids. And get over it. But Larry League was a teacher in his forties when he was struck down with dinophilia: 'Dinosaurs were not the "in" thing when I was a child … I've collected rocks, minerals and fossils all my life, but there were few dinosaur remains in Kansas where I lived. After obtaining a professorship in North Dakota, I was living near dinosaur-bearing strata. Having my summers free from teaching I began searching for dinosaurs …'

Mr League was extraordinarily lucky. While hunting in the Hell Creek Formation of Dakota and Montana, he found a nearly complete Triceratops skeleton and other bones from many different Late Cretaceous dinosaurs – rich pickings indeed for a beginner.

The idea of the Dakota Dinosaur Museum first originated in 1987 when Larry League's personal collection began to exceed several thousand specimens. With the city providing the building funds, Larry and his wife Alice coordinated the development, fundraising and construction of the 1,250-square-metre (13,400-square-foot) museum, which today runs on its gift-shop takings and entrance fees.

The doors opened in May 1994. And Mr League struck lucky again. The first *Jurassic Park* movie was released at the same time. Mr League recalls: 'It was dinomania for about three years. People wanted to see the dinosaurs that were in the movie so we added new dinosaur sculptures like Velociraptor and "Compy" Compsognathus to our collection.'

Today the Dakota Dinosaur Museum features eleven full-scale dinosaurs, including the real skeleton of a Triceratops inside a 'Triassic-Cretaceous time continuum', plus three full-scale dinos out of doors. There are full-scale skeletal casts – replicas of real bones of the Allosaurus, Albertosaurus, Thescelosaurus and Stegosaurus. New in 2006 is a four-foot baby Tyrannosaurus rex. Visitors can also view a complete Triceratops skull in the museum's model lab, and a colourful collection of minerals including pink terlingua calcite from Mexico, eerie white hydrozincite from Nevada and brilliant blue fluorite from England.

The Leagues themselves work at the museum daily, so visitors are able to talk with the person who actually collected the specimens. This is, of course, one of the joys of small, specialist museums – being able to discuss the items and their discovery, and put questions personally to someone who has all the answers, and all the passion and enthusiasm to answer them well.

Mr League explains: 'It's hard for people to grasp geologic time and the fact that North Dakota once had a subtropical climate with an ocean and sandy shoreline, an ideal setting for dinosaur activity.'

Everyone has a favourite dinosaur. Most go for the heavy-weights like T. rex. But Mr League is loyal to Triceratops: 'I think many people like Triceratops because its unique three-horned head is easy to recognise.'

There is also a dinosaur museum in Frick, Switzerland, and Dinosaur World at Colwyn Bay, Wales. There's Styrassic Park in Bad Gleichenberg, Austria, with life-size models in an outdoor setting. Then there's the Wyoming Dinosaur Center and Dig Sites, the Devil's Coulee Dinosaur Heritage Museum in Alberta, Canada, the original nesting site of Hadrosaur (duckbill) dinosaurs. The museum features a Hadrosaur nest and embryo. In South Africa, there's the Sudwala Dinosaur Park ... to mention but a few.

THE GALLERY OF MONSTER TOYS

Online at www.thegalleryofmonstertoys.com

'Vintage monster toys ... are humble and imperfect. They depict flawed, tortured creatures. These toys capture a time when horror was fun.' Raymond Castile, curator

This seriously scary online museum is dedicated to the monsters of a more innocent past, the creaking stars of early special effects, creatures fashioned before computer art, and hand-modelled from bits of rubber and metal. These are the monsters that haunted the imaginations of a whole generation of baby-boomers, starring in creature features and chiller theatres. Welcome back, Godzilla! Well hello, Wolf Man! Nice to see you again, Creature from the Black Lagoon!

There are four wings in this museum, each devoted to a different decade of monster toys. The curator, Raymond Castile, knows his subject inside out, and explains how the development of different monster trends was shaped by the changing faces of popular entertainment, mass psychology, retail and technology. The collections are arranged according to manufacturer, as monster formats tended to be sold in series. Mr Castile goes into marketing, packaging, design – all without for one moment losing his sense of humour. Different products featured include model kits, plastic figures, battery-operated moving monsters and 'soakies' (bubble-bath containers shaped as monsters).

Forgotten stars of the toybox include the Aurora House of Horrors Guillotine (complete with body) from 1964. This model-making company was ahead of its time, consulting child psychologists before launching its monster series on the market.

Louis Marx & Co. created some of the best battery-operated toys that ever walked the tabletop. Thanks to them, children of the 1960s could play with a 30-centimetre (12-inch) remote-control Frankenstein, a plush Yeti with a bloodcurdling shriek and a Mighty Kong who beat his furry chest. Not to mention 'the Great Garloo', a 60-centimetre-tall (2-foot) bug-eyed green creature who shuddered around and was equipped with a formidable gripping action.

Godzilla had started his toy career in Japan in the 1960s but he didn't take off in America until the 1970s. Toy manufacturers Mattel improved on the movie original – *their* toy could shoot off its right hand like a missile. Mattel also released a monster Rodan as a counterpart for Godzilla. This huge toy had a 1-metre (38-inch) wingspan. Mr Castile comments: 'The Mattel Rodan stands out as one of the best, and most under-appreciated toys of the 1970s.'

Another star of the collection is the 1979 Kenner Alien ('One of the most sought-after, highly regarded action figures ever made', according to Mr Castile). Strangely popular with children, despite being the star of an 'R' rated film, the Kenner Alien stood 45 centimetres (18 inches) tall. A transparent dome revealed glow-in-the-dark skull and brains. At the touch of a button the Alien retracted its jaws.

Mr Castile grew up reading *Famous Monsters of Filmland*, a magazine edited by Forrest J. Ackerman. His own monstermania grew from its pages. On the website, the curator touchingly describes his pilgrimage to the 'Ackermansion', a mecca for monster fans. The 'Ackermonster' took him on a guided tour.

In his FAQs, the curator patiently explains that he is not a dealer, gives advice on finding vintage monsters, and reveals his favourites.

THE JELL-O MUSEUM

23 East Main Street, Le Roy, New York 14482, USA
Telephone: (USA 001) 585 768 7433
www.jellomuseum.com

'If you've ever wondered what the human brain and Jell-O have in common – you'll find the answer at the Jell-O Museum.'

Lynne Belluscio, director

We'll put you out of your misery immediately on the first question. Mind-wobbling but true – on 17 March 1993, technicians at St Jerome hospital in Batavia tested a bowl of lime Jell-O with an EEG machine and confirmed that a bowl of Jell-O has electrical waves identical to those of the brains of human adults. Ever creative in the marketing department, the Jell-O Museum store now sells brain-shaped moulds, thoughtfully providing for both large brains and small ones.

The museum, opened to mark Jell-O's centenary in 1997, displays 100 years of production and marketing history. A museum devoted to Jell-O might not seem so significant, but the makers of the 'delicate, delightful, dainty' dessert were outstanding champions and pioneers in the art of advertising. In some ways the history of Jell-O is the history of the true art of marketing. The simple gelatin dessert spawned not just catchphrases, such as 'There's Always Room for Jell-O', but also the concept of a mascot, of celebrity spokespersons, of subtle marketing using recipe books in which the product was always a key ingredient.

Jell-O was the first to send well-trained, well-groomed salesmen on the road in 'spanking rigs, drawn by beautiful horses' to advertise their product at fairs, country gatherings, church socials and parties. Then came team-drawn wagons, followed by smart cars.

Jell-O made itself seen and known in posters and billboards over the American landscape, as well as in magazines and newspapers. Jell-O drew on the skills of top artists of the time for their publicity. Among the exhibits in the museum are twenty original oil paintings commissioned from the likes of Rose O'Neill, Maxfield Parrish and Norman Rockwell.

In 1904, Jell-O introduced the Jell-O Girl. The model was Elizabeth King, daughter of an artist who worked for the company's advertising agency. In 1934 Jack Benny was signed up for the cause, and the whole world came to know 'J-E-L-L-O'. Bill Cosby has been Jell-O's spokesperson since 1974.

Where did it all begin? In 1897, Pearle Wait, a carpenter in Le Roy, ran a sideline in cough remedies and laxative tea. He experimented with gelatin and came up with a fruit-flavoured dessert which his wife, May, named Jell-O. It tasted delicious, but Mr Wait did not know how to spread the good news. In 1899 he sold his formula for $450 to one Orator Woodward, a successful manufacturer but above all marketer of a remedy for hen-lice and Grain-O, a coffee substitute.

At first Jell-O performed miserably and had to be carried by the success of Grain-O. But the very first Jell-O advertising campaign in 1900 transformed the dessert's fortunes, bringing sales up to an astonishing $250,000 a year. From that moment Jell-O became not just a dessert but a marketing phenomenon.

On 31 December 1925 the Jell-O Company, Inc. was sold to the Postum Cereal Company, Inc., becoming the first subsidiary of what would eventually become General Foods Corporation. Today Jell-O is manufactured by Kraft/General Foods in Dover, Delaware.

The museum store bulges with Jell-O merchandise. The visitor (also online) can buy boxer shorts with Jell-O's marketing word-bites: 'Watch it Wiggle – See it Jiggle.'

THE WAX MUSEUM

Piazza dei Santi Apostoli 67, 00187 Rome, Italy

Telephone: (Italy 0039) 06 679 6482

www.museodellecere.it

*'Between ourselves and our real natures we interpose that wax
figure of idealisations and selections which we call our character.'*

Walter Lippmann

Wax museums invariably seem slightly sinister. Rome's little waxworks is the only one that has a kind of ramshackle loveability. Maybe it's because all the 160 figures seem to have disproportionately large heads, and ears like Prince Charles, or because many of the exhibits appear to wear the same black patent leather shoes, be they Lucrezia Borgia or Mussolini.

The museum was brought to 'life' in 1958 by Fernando Canini, who visited Madame Tussaud's in London and Gravin's in Paris. He came home determined to give Italy's capital something to be proud of. Indeed, this collection is number one in Italy when it comes to the number of wax figures, and third in Europe.

Ten rooms show figures *a grandezza naturale* (life-size) arranged in interesting tableaux. Leonardo da Vinci paints the Mona Lisa – in the company of the Medici family and Niccolò Macchiavelli. Around a roulette table in Venice we see the famous charlatan Count Cagliostro, Lucrezia and Cesare Borgia and Madame Pompadour, mistress of Louis XV of France.

There's an emphasis on Italian characters, including Padre Pio, Victor Emmanuel II, Camillo Benso di Cavour and, of course, Nero.

From the world of art, there are Michelangelo, Goya and Picasso. Literature is represented by Oscar Wilde and Lord Byron (who lived in Italy for many years), as well as Dante and Leopardi. From the annals of musical history, the museum offers Strauss, Toscanini, Verdi, Wagner and Puccini. There are modern singers too – Italian pop groups Totti, Nesta, and i Pooh. From the world of fairytales, there's *Bianca Neve* (Snow-White) and *i sette nani* (seven dwarves) and *la Bella Addormentata* (Sleeping Beauty). Thrown in, without any explanation, is a tank of colourful china dinosaurs. A small *Camera degli Orrori* features a garrotte, an electric chair and a gas chamber.

Speaking of horrors, Fascist leaders feature heavily in this museum. There are wax effigies of Adolf Hitler, Heinrich Himmler and 'Giuseppe' Stalin. To be fair, you can also see Winston Churchill, Roosevelt and Mao Tse Tung.

The most chilling assemblage of all is a complete reproduction of the last day that Mussolini held the reins of Italy, everyone around the table wearing grim expressions. This was the last meeting of the Grand Council of Fascism that took place on 25 July 1943.

There are many other wax museums in the world but none has quite the special charm of this one, so unexpected in sophisticated Rome.

THE MARY AND MARVIN JOHNSON
GOURD MUSEUM

The Municipal Building, 28 North Raleigh
Street, Angier, North Carolina 27501, USA
Telephone: (USA 001) 919 639 2071

'If you give or receive a gourd,
with it goes all the best in life:
health, happiness and other good things.'

A framed poem on the wall of
the original gourd museum

When Marvin Johnson planned to grow a true champion gourd, he would dynamite a crater and fill it with rotted sawdust and chicken manure. Over his lifetime, he was to grow more than 200 kinds, from bushels strong enough for a grown man to stand on, to dippers taller than he was.

Given such fierce enthusiasm for what some call the earliest crop, it's not surprising that Marvin Johnson served for many years as president of what is now the North Carolina Gourd Society (established in 1937).

He started the original Mary and Marvin Johnson Gourd Museum in the woods behind his farm in 1964, after his wife Mary complained that his private collection was crowding the human inhabitants out of their home. So he built a little white house for the gourds amid a wildflower garden created by Mary.

Mr Johnson had grown up with gourds. He recalled: 'We used dippers to drink from. We'd tie two gourds together and use them to swim with. My mother raised them, and we boys carried them up under the tin roof to dry.'

The first gourds he grew on his farm were the small, colourful ornamental variety. This was because children always wanted to play with them – and because the women liked them, he said. Most of the gourds in the museum collection, however, are durable hardshells, and they come from all over the world.

The names of some gourds reflect their uses by humans: the African wine kettle, sugar trough or tobacco box, for example. Marvin Johnson's gourds include many reshaped and redecorated for tasks and leisure, using techniques such as carving, burning, painting and the addition of materials such as metal, leather and beads.

There's a Masai blood collector, various dolls, birdhouses and containers of many kinds. Some gourds are cut in half to become display cases like miniature theatres for tiny dioramas. There are gourds of Christmas carol singers, ice-skaters and religious scenes.

Other gourds found their way to this museum simply because they look very much like something else – a swan, a dog or a bird, or even Benjamin Franklin. Natural characteristics are emphasised with paintwork and accessories – thus a long-necked gourd becomes a cat playing the violin or Popeye.

Some of the earliest gourds to come to the museum were from the collection of the now defunct New England Gourd Society, a predecessor of the American Gourd Society. Appreciative gourd-crafters also contributed their work to the museum. Visitors can see a gourd penguin, dolls, a rattlesnake, a kaleidoscope and a whole orchestra carved out of gourds, including a miniature piano. Connie Troutman turned Marvin's basketball gourds into pierced lanterns to light the museum. Ralph Schneider created a duplicate of a gourd elephant he presented to Richard Nixon and built a coal-fired train complete with engineer. New Zealand artist Theo Schoon sent gourds carved in Maori patterns and seasoned in volcanic mud springs.

Outside the museum there used to be one unusual exhibit: a live alligator, which Marvin Johnson hand-fed with hot dogs. The gator, which was, of course, immortalised on a painted gourd, lived nearly twenty years outside the museum until it was apparently shot by hunters.

Marvin Johnson himself passed away in 2002. His gourd collection went to the Kennebec Baptist Church and eventually found a new home in the Angier Municipal Building in 2006.

THE CLOWN'S GALLERY-MUSEUM

All Saints Centre, Haggerston Road, Hackney,
London E8 4HT, England
Telephone: (UK 0044) (0)870 128 4336
www.clowns-international.co.uk

'Pro funnibono publico'

Clowns International's original motto

Nothing's more ephemeral than a laugh. So the clowns of the world have found a unique way to immortalise themselves. They get their portraits painted in 'full slap' (make-up and costume) – on an egg.

The egg register serves a practical purpose. It's a kind of clown copyright service, servicing an unwritten rule (known as 'the Code') that one clown never copies the make-up of another. A clown's name also dies with him, as does his unique costume.

The egg-portrait tradition started just after the Second World War, when Stan Bult, founder of the International Circus Clowns Club, started recording the faces of his colleagues on blown chicken eggs. The collection grew in size and fame. By 1951 it was on display at the Centenary Exhibition at Crystal Palace, and was lent out to other venues.

Travelling eggs are vulnerable, and some of the early portraits were sadly lost in unfortunate curatorial accidents. But succeeding generations of clowns continue the tradition. The portraits are now painted on more durable pottery eggs. The current egg artist is Kate Stone, who ensures total accuracy using samples of wig hair and costume swatches. Every member of Clowns International receives an egg voucher on joining, and when they have established their face they submit their images for an egg portrait. The results can now be seen at the Clown's Gallery-Museum in London.

Apart from over 225 eggs (including 24 from the original collection, recently recovered), the museum contains costumes, props, photos, books and statues. (The collection's growing all the time, as clowns often will their own effects to the museum.) There's a display about Joseph Grimaldi, Britain's most famous clown, who pioneered lead-free make-up and hence healthy clowning. Also a recording of Coco the Clown, talking about road safety, his great cause. Coco was inspired by a devoted young fan who was hurt in a car accident. The gallery boasts a statue of Coco and his original walking stick. There are also statues of Charlie Cairoli and his white-faced partner, Paulo.

The gallery is run by clowns, who are only too happy to answer questions. It is, as curator Mattie Faint explains, 'a living archive to a unique profession'. Congenitally unable to resist a bit of clowning, he adds: 'Come along and talk to the people in the nose.'

In the nose, they certainly are. Did you, for example, know that the term 'ham acting' is based on a make-up recipe of pig-fat and powder?

Mattie (who's been clowning for 37 years and is Clown Number 36 in the egg collection) gives short shrift to the myth that clowns are sad or scary. 'That old chestnut! We're here to spread sunshine and happiness.' He, like many of his colleagues, works as a 'clown-doctor', visiting children's hospitals in London.

Clowns International is now a worldwide body that promotes clowning, clown festivals and clown history, and even runs a benevolent fund to help clowns fallen on hard times. A highlight of their year is the Joseph Grimaldi memorial service, held the first Sunday of February in London at the Clown's Church, Holy Trinity, Beechwood Road, Dalston. Wreaths are laid for Grimaldi and any clowns who have gone up to the Big Top in the sky during the past year. However, the occasion is far from solemn, as the service is conducted in full costume and attended by the local schoolchildren bearing candles.

THE NATIONAL LIAR'S HALL OF FAME

The 'Lille' Mermaid, 106 South Mill Street,
Dannebrog, Nebraska 68831, USA
Telephone: (USA 001) 308 226 2222
www.dannebrog.org

'A unique collection of oddball items that have no earthly function than to generate a good laugh.'

Gaylord Mickelsen, executive curator

You can't actually believe anything you see in this museum. The man who set it up is an expert in tall tales, his exhibits all purport to be what they're not, and even the statistics bandied about concerning the museum itself are quite certainly untrue.

Roger Welsch (aka 'Captain Nebraska') is the museum's founder. By his own admission, Welsch specialises in 'prevarication and metric mendacity'.

The former TV presenter will, for example, happily tell you that his National Liar's Hall of Fame is regularly compared with the Smithsonian, and that tours for more than 500 visitors are free.

Five hundred visitors might stretch the resources of this tiny museum in the picturesque little town of Dannebrog, Nebraska. Dannebrog is the name of the flag of Denmark, from where many of the town's first settlers hailed. Dannebrog proudly proclaims itself the Danish capital of Nebraska.

In one of his many incarnations, Welsch is the author of books about subjects ranging from old tractors to dogs, edible wild plants and sod houses. He's even turned his talents to food:

Diggin' in and Piggin' out: the Truth about Food and Men (HarperCollins, 1997). But Nebraska and his hometown are his number one passions. His feelings are clearly reciprocated: the main thoroughfare through Dannebrog is called Roger Welsch Avenue.

The museum was launched in 1986. Roger Welsch explains that it all started with the photos of US presidents Johnson, Nixon and Washington in a local tavern. 'The bartender explained to me that Washington never told a lie, Johnson never told the truth, and Nixon didn't know the difference.'

He adds ruefully: 'The current crowd of thieves running things wouldn't know the truth if it slapped them in the ass with a board.'

These days his museum is situated inside the Lille Mermaid gift shop. Among a select group of exhibits there's a fly-swatter with a big hole in the middle. This is displayed alongside its certificates from the Occupational Safety and Health Administrator and the Society for the Prevention of Cruelty to Flies.

There's a box of painted golf balls, curated as 'Golf Balls as Big as Hail'. The Nebraska Cornhuskers have 'contributed' a football signed by all the team. It's covered in simple Xs. There's a two-way hammer, grow-your-own cow seeds (to grow your own), and an electric nose-picker.

As a professional folklorist, the kind of lies that really interest Mr Welsch are the ones that laugh at life and say something about the human condition – more tall tales than falsehoods. For example: 'It's so cold, I saw a politician with his hands in his own pockets.'

Is Mr Welsch a talented liar himself? 'I am a scholar. I only repeat what I have heard. Sometimes I am shocked to find that I have been told untruths.'

Who's Mr Welsch's Number One Liar? 'The Baron von Munchhausen of course was most famous ... but frankly, any husband coming home after two in the morning with beer on his breath and lipstick on his collar is an instant contender.'

But remember this information comes from a man who claims that everything he knows about women he learned from his tractor. For more information on this, see his 1998 book, *Old Tractors and the Men Who Love Them: How to Keep Your Family Running and Your Tractor Happy.*

Longlist

Other unusual museums and where to find them:

THE ARTS & ENTERTAINMENT

The Cartoon Museum, London, England

The Museum of the Art of Flamenco, Jerez de la Frontera, Spain

The National Four String Banjo Hall of Fame Museum, Guthrie, Oklahoma, USA

The Edith Piaf Museum, Paris, France

The Faust Museum, Knittlingen, Baden-Württemberg, Germany

The Stradivarius Museum, Cremona, Italy

The Trumpet Museum, Bad Säckingen, Germany

The Organ Museum, Borgentreich, Germany

The Johnson Victrola Museum, Dover, Delaware, USA

The Jules Verne Museum, Nantes, France

The Museum of Forbidden Art, Berlin, Germany

The National Music Museum, the University of South Dakota, USA

The Laurel and Hardy Museum, Ulverston, England

The Anne of Green Gables Museum, Prince Edward Island, Canada

The Liberace Museum, Las Vegas, Nevada, USA

The Barney Smith Toilet Seat Art Museum, Alamo Heights, Texas, USA

The Barnum Museum (dedicated to the famous showman), Bridgeport, Connecticut, USA

The Museum of the Moving Image, Queens, New York, USA

The Playing Card Museum, Turnhout, Belgium

FOOD & DRINK

The Gourmet Museum of Oh! Forgotten Vegetables, Sadirac, France

The House of Wheat and Bread, Echallens, Switzerland

The German Bread Museum, Ulm, Germany

The Bread Museum, Charenton-le-Pont, France

The Potato Museum, Fussgonheim, Germany

The Potato Dumpling Museum, Heichelheim, Weimar, Germany

The Wyandot Popcorn Museum, Marion, Ohio, USA

The Instant Ramen Invention Museum, Ikeda-city, Japan

The Orange Museum, Borriana, Castellón, Spain

The National Apple Museum, Biglerville, Pennsylvania, USA

The Museum of Plums and Prunes, Agen, France

The International Banana Club Museum, Hesperia, California, USA

The Banana Museum, Sainte-Marie, Martinique

The Museum of the Strawberry, Wépion, Belgium

The Sugar Museum, Berlin, Germany

The Maffra Sugar Beet Museum and Robotic Dairy Interpretive Centre, Victoria, Australia

The Peppermint Museum, Eichenau, Germany

The Burlingame Museum of Pez [peppermint dispenser] Memorabilia, California, USA

The Museum of Honey, Trento, Italy (one of dozens of honey museums around the world)

The Museum of the History and Development of Chocolate, Berlin, Germany

The Chocolate Museum, Cologne, Germany

The Museum of the Olive Tree, Imperia, Italy

The Cyclades Olive Museum, Andros Island, Greece

Spicy's Gewürzmuseum (Museum of Spices), Hamburg, Germany

The Hungarian Paprika Museum, Kalocsa, Hungary

The Horseradish Museum, Baiersdorf, Nuremberg, Germany

The Kimch'i Field Museum, Seoul, Korea

The International Vinegar Museum, Roslyn, South Dakota, USA

The Oscar Getz Museum of Whiskey History, Kentucky, USA

The Grappa Museum, Bassano del Grappa (Vicenza), Italy

The Guinness Museum, Dublin, Ireland

The Vodka Museum, Moscow, Russia

The Schmidt Museum of Coca-Cola® Memorabilia, Elizabethtown, Kentucky, USA

The Museum of the Chestnut, Pescaglia Colognora, Italy

The Eco-Museum of the Truffle, Sorges, France

The Eco-Museum of the Perigord Walnut, Castelnaud-la-Chapelle, France

The National Foie Gras Museum, Thiviers, France (one of at least four foie gras museums in France; others at Frespech, Samatan and Roquettes)

The Museum of Ham, Madrid, Spain

The International Hamburger Hall of Fame, Daytona Beach, Florida, USA

The Hamburger Hall of Fame, Seymour, Wisconsin, USA

Colonel Harland Sanders Café and Museum, Corbin, Kentucky, USA (and the Colonel Harland Sanders Museum in Louisville, Kentucky, USA)

The Catfish Museum, Belzoni, Mississippi, USA

The Museum of Oysters, Charente-Maritime, France (others at Marennes and at Bourcefranc-le-Chapus, France)

The Dutch Cheese Museum, Alkmaar, the Netherlands

The Museum of Jam, Pau, France

The Museum of Camembert, Vimoutiers, France

The German Cookery Book Museum, Dortmund, Germany

The Grocery Museum, Vancouver, Canada

The Cookie Jar Museum, Lemont, Illinois, USA

The American Diner Museum, Providence, Rhode Island, USA

The Museum of Brands, Packaging and Advertising, London, England

The World's Largest Collection of Rare Porcelain *Veilleuses Théières* (night-light teapots), Trenton, Tennessee, USA

SHOES & FASHION

The Bertolini Museum of Shoemaking, Vigevano, Italy

The Shoe Museum, Barcelona, Spain, (others at Romans, France, Woolwijk, the Netherlands and Philadelphia, Pennsylvania, USA)

The Leather and Shoe Museum, Offenbach am Main, Germany

The Bata Shoe Museum, Ontario, Canada

The Museum of Shoes and Sporting Footwear, Montebelluna, Italy

The Sock Museum, Yokohama, Japan

Leila's Hair Museum, Independence, Missouri, USA

The Scottish Tartans Museum, Comrie, Scotland

The Museum of Umbrellas and Parasols, Gignese, Italy

The Museum of Felt, Mouzon, France

The Bridal Museum, Saint-Joachim, France

The Victorian Wedding Museum, Kenton, Ohio, USA

The Museum of Perfume, Grasse, France

The Fan Museum, London, England

The National Eyeglasses Museum, Amsterdam, the
Netherlands

The Tattoo Museum and Tattoo Studio, Amsterdam, the
Netherlands

The Miller Comb Museum, Homer, Alaska, USA

History & Social History

The Museum of the Visigoths, Toledo, Spain

The Conspiracy Museum, Dallas, Texas, USA

The Sixth Floor Museum (at 411 Elm Street – the bullets that
killed J.F. Kennedy were allegedly fired from here), Dallas,
Texas, USA

The Workhouse Museum of Poor Law, Ripon, North
Yorkshire, England

The Famine Museum, Strokestown, Ireland

The Dortmond Museum of Handwriting, the Netherlands

The Foreign Legion Museum, Aubagne, France

The Tolpuddle Martyr Museum, Dorchester, Dorset, England

The Luftwaffe Museum, Appen, Germany

The Gay Men's History Museum, Berlin, Germany

The Museum of Smuggling History, Ventnor, Isle of Wight,
England

The Great Blacks in Wax Museum, Baltimore, Maryland, USA

The Fort Fürigen Museum of War History, Stansstad,
  Switzerland

The Inflation Museum, Cologne, Germany

The Trash Museum, Hartford, Connecticut, USA

The Shipwreck Museum, Cuxhaven, Germany (there's also the
  Shipwreck Heritage Centre at Hastings, England)

The Stasi Museum, Leipzig, Germany

The Museum of Crime and Criminals, Zürich, Switzerland

The National Cryptologic Museum, Fort George Meade,
  Maryland, USA

The Bandit Museum, Ronda, Spain

The Diefenbunker, Canada's Cold War Museum, Ottawa,
  Canada

The Prague Torture Museum, Czech Republic

The Jim Crow Museum of Racist Memorabilia, Ferris State
  University, Big Rapids, Michigan, USA

The Museum of the Illegal Party Printing Works, Belgrade,
  Serbia

The Valentine Museum, Quincy, Illinois, USA

SCIENCE, TECHNOLOGY & MEDICINE

The Leitz Collection of Historic Microscopes, Wetzlar,
  Germany

The Petroleum Museum, Wietze, Germany

The National Atomic Museum, Albuquerque, New Mexico,
  USA

The Atomic Testing Museum, Las Vegas, Nevada, USA

The Shovel Museum, North Easton, Maryland, USA

The Arkansas Oil and Brine Museum, Smackover, Arkansas,
  USA

The Kansas Barbed Wire Museum, La Crosse, Kansas, USA

The Wimbledon Windmill Museum, London, England

The Remington Firearms Museum and County Store, Ilion, New York, USA

The UFO Enigma Museum, Roswell, New Mexico, USA

The Hammer Museum, Haines, Alaska, USA

The Volkswagen Museum, Wolfsburg, Germany

The Museum of Carts, Filottrano, Italy

The National Lighter Museum, Guthrie, Oklahoma, USA

The Pennsylvania Trolley Museum, Washington, Pennsylvania, USA

The National Museum of Musical Clocks to Street Organs, Utrecht, the Netherlands

The Manuel da Maia Museum of Water, Lisbon, Portugal

The Museum of Counterfeits, Paris, France

The Vacuum Cleaner Museum, Portland, Oregon, USA

The Museum of Edged Weapons and Cutlery, Solingen, Germany

The Cement Works Museum, Maceira-Liz, Portugal

The Museum of Tugs and Towing, Maassluis, the Netherlands

The Antique Fan Collectors' Museum, Andover, Kansas, USA

The Museum of Locks and Hardware, Velbert, Germany

The World Brick Museum, Maizuru, Japan

Porter's Thermometer Museum, Onset, Massachusetts, USA

The Cumberland Pencil Museum, Keswick, Cumbria, England

Bill Dalley's Windmill Collection, Portales, New Mexico, USA

The Museum of Bells, Annecy-le-Vieux, France

The Sikkens Museum of Signs, The Hague, the Netherlands

The Museum of Coaches, Leek, the Netherlands

The Colour Museum, Bradford, England

The German Museum of Firefighting, Fulda, Germany

The Matchstick Museum, Tomar, Portugal

The Helicopter Museum, Weston-super-Mare, England

The Museum of Holography, Chicago, Illinois, USA

The Museum of Knots and Sailors' Ropework, Ipswich, Suffolk, England

The Dorus Rijkers Museum of Lifesaving, Den Helder, the Netherlands

The Kenneth W. Berger Hearing Aid Museum, Kent State University, Ohio, USA

The Museum of Vision, San Francisco, California, USA

The German X-Ray Museum, Remscheid, Germany

The German Epilepsy Museum, Kork, Germany

The Leprosy Museum, Bergen, Norway

The Wilhelm Reich Museum, Rangeley, Maine, USA

The Glore Psychiatric Museum, St Joseph, Missouri, USA

The Museum of the Human Hand, Lausanne, Switzerland

The Mütter Museum (of human medical anomalies), Philadelphia, Pennsylvania, USA

The Tactual Museum of the Lighthouse for the Blind, Kallithea, Greece

The Nose Academy (part of the Museum of Student Life), Lund, Sweden

The Museum of Death, San Diego, California, USA

FOLKLORE & TRADITION

The Museum of the Brothers Grimm, Kassel, Germany

The National Museum of Nativity Scenes, Rome, Italy

The Museum of Nativity Cribs, Prague, Czech Republic

The Aluminium Tree and Ornament Museum, Brevard, North
  Carolina, USA

The Bullfight Museum, Barcelona, Spain (and another in
  Valencia, Spain)

The German Museum of Fairytales, Bad Oeynhausen, Germany

Toys & Childhood

The Barbie Museum, Helsinki, Finland

The Angels Attic Museum (of dolls and dolls' houses) Santa
  Monica, California, USA

The Toy Train Museum, Strasburg, Pennsylvania, USA

The Oz Museum, Wamego, Kansas, USA

The Marionette Museum, Stockholm, Sweden

The Museum of Automata, Souillac, France

The Teddy Bear Museum, Naples, Florida, USA

The 'World of Steiff' Teddy Bear Museum, Giengen, Germany

The Struwwelpeter Museum, Frankfurt-am-Main, Germany

The National Farm Toy Museum, Dyersville, Iowa, USA

The German Museum of Tin Figures, Kulmbach, Germany

The Spinning Top Exploratory Museum, Burlington,
  Wisconsin, USA

The Ragged School Museum, London, England

The Children's Garbage Museum, Stratford, Connecticut, USA

The Uncle Remus Museum, Eatonton, Georgia, USA

The Foundling Museum, London, England

The Merry-Go-Round Museum, Sandusky, Ohio, USA

Pollock's Toy Museum, London, England

Reverend Jen's Troll Museum (toy trolls), New York City, USA

SPORT

The Lawn-Tennis Museum, London, England

The National Museum of Roller Skating, Lincoln, Nebraska, USA

The Somerset Cricket Museum, Taunton, England

The World Kite Museum, Long Beach, Washington, USA

The Dog Mushing [sledding] Museum, Fairbanks, Alaska, USA

The American Museum of Fly Fishing, Manchester, Vermont, USA

The National Bowling Hall of Fame and Museum, St Louis, Missouri, USA

The Bugatti Trust, Cheltenham, Gloucestershire, England

The Safari Museum, Chanute, Kansas, USA

The Santa Cruz Surfing Museum, California, USA

The California Surf Museum, Oceanside, California, USA

The Canberra Bicycle Museum, ACT, Australia

The Museum of Rugby, London, England

The International Balloon and Airship Museum, Mitchell, South Dakota, USA

NATURE

The US National Tick Collection, Statesborough, Georgia, USA

The Little Museum of the Bird's Nest and Feeding Trough, Brussels, Belgium

The American International Rattlesnake Museum, Albuquerque, New Mexico, USA

The Finch-Catching Museum, Harelbeke, Belgium

The Welsh Slate Museum, Gwynedd, Wales

The National Dragonfly Museum, Ashton, England

The Museum of Petrification, Savonnières, France

The Official Loch Ness Monster Exhibition Centre (and the Original Loch Ness Monster Exhibition), Drumnadrochit, Scotland

The Dormouse Museum, Cerknica, Slovenia

The Owl Art and Craft Museum, Seoul, Korea

The Museum of Dirt, Boston, Massachusetts, USA

The Permafrost Museum, Igarka, Russia

The Museum of Rose Oil, Kazanluk, Bulgaria

The World Famous Gopher Hole Museum, Torrington, Alberta, Canada

MISCELLANEOUS

The Dog Museum, Berlin, Germany and St Louis, Missouri, USA

The Dog Collar Museum, Maidstone, Kent, England

The Oakham Castle Horse Shoe Collection, Oakham, Rutland, England

Carr's One of a Kind Museum (celebrity vintage cars), Spokane, Washington, USA

The Museum of Magic and Curiosity, Paris, France

The Houdini Historical Center, Appleton, Wisconsin, USA

The Wallpaper Museum, Rixheim, France

The Time Museum, Rockford, Illinois, USA

The Decoy Duck Museum, Havre de Grace, Maryland, USA

Creation Evidence Museum, Glen Rose, Texas, USA

The Nutcracker Museum, Leavenworth, Washington, USA

Steve's Weird House, Seattle, Washington, USA

The Rose Museum, Bad Nauheim, Germany

The Squished Penny Museum, Washington DC, USA

The Exotic World Burlesque Hall of Fame, Helendale, California, USA

The Vent Haven Ventriloquism Museum, Fort Mitchell, Kentucky, USA

Ripley's Believe It or Not! Museums – 24 locations worldwide, but best known in Hollywood, California, USA

The Newseum, Interactive Museum of News, Washington DC, USA

The 'Silent Night' Museum (about the Christmas carol), Oberndorf bei Salzburg, Austria

Some Recommended Virtual Museums

Messages from another world chronicled with witty comments at www.weirdfortunecookies.com

Neon from the 1940s to the present at www.neonmuseum.org (the physical museum should open in 2008)

The Museum of Obscure Patents at www.ipwatchdog.com/patentmuseum.html

Photographs of American ghost towns at www.ghosttown gallery.com

'Why Cats Paint?' and other similarly arch questions answered at the Museum of Non-Primate Art at www.monpa.com

UFOs and Yetis, speculation and conspiracy, at the Museum of Unnatural Mystery at www.unmuseum.org

Unspeakable vintage recipe books eviscerated at the Gallery of Regrettable Food at www.lileks.com

Diagrams, explanations, history at the Museum of Unworkable Devices at www.lhup.edu/~dsimanek/museum/unwork.htm

A million pages of transcripts, documents, photos from the Nuremberg Trials at http://nuremberg.law.harvard.edu

Unnatural animals at www.roguetaxidermy.com

Financial scams and frauds uncovered at www.quatloos.com

The history and practice of Ouija boards at www.museumof talkingboards.com

All about the short-lived English Queen, Lady Jane Grey at www.bitterwisdom.com/ladyjanegrey

Sob stories at www.garden-gnomes-need-homes.com

The Virtual Toilet Paper Museum at http://nobodys-perfect.com

The World Famous Asphalt Museum at http://ecs.csus.edu/~ gordonvs/asphalt/asphalt.htm

What the comic book superheroes snack on at www.geocities. com/superherofood

Everything about the Green Fairy drink and the effects it conjures at the Virtual Absinthe Museum at www.oxygenee. com

The Museum of Bathtub Art – an online gallery at www.bath tubmuseum.org

Cypress knee sculptures (cypress knees are a knotty part of the root system of the cypress tree) at www.kozmicdreams.com/ tomgaskins

Collectors' items at www.toastermuseum.com

A comprehensive photographic record, seriously curated at www.toycannons.ray-vin.com

The Cyberspace Vintage Vacuum Cleaner Museum at www.137.com/museum

The museum of buttons at www.buttonarium.com

The Virtual Valve Museum at http://valve.museum.com

Lettuces with faces, a banana chip with a likeness of the Virgin Mary and Something Nasty in the Ramen at the Museum of Food Anomalies at www.hanttula.com/exhibits/freakyfood

Dr Darren's World of Crabs at www.brachyura.fsnet.co.uk

Josephine Baker to Mental as Anything and other banana-related imagery and anecdotes at the Washington Banana Museum at www.bananamuseum.com

The Museum of Online Museums at www.coudal.com/moom. php

The Museum of Coat Hangers at homepage.mac.com/marches
baugh/moch/intro

A psychedelic meditation on philosophy, art and fashion at
www.hippiemuseum.org

Fashion history, care and culture of the famous German
leather pants at www.lederhosenmuseum.de

Drinks, mixology and chat at www.museumoftheamerican
cocktail.org

How to classify very small objects, plus exhibits at www.very
smallobjects.com

The Museum of Old Soviet Radios at oldradio.onego.ru/foy.htm

Batman, Latin-American style at www.batmania.com

The Antique Mouse and Rat Trap Gallery at http://people.hws.
edu/cicciarelli/trapic1.html

The Ahmet Sonmez Collection of Old Razor Blades at
www.antrak.org.tr

The Museum of Weird Books at www.pistilbooks.com/
museum/museum09.html

Photos and explanations at the Online Tornado Museum at
http://members.aol.com/tornadfoto

Freaks, 'fartistes' and far-out oddities at www.thehuman
marvels.com

Loveable mascots from the past at the Orphanage of Cast-Off
[Advertising] Orphans at www.lileks.com

Interior Desecrations, Horrible Homes from the Brass Age of
American Design at www.lileks.com

The Online Potato Museum at www.potatomuseum.com

Diets, collectibles and fashions better forgotten in the Bad
Fads Museum at www.badfads.com

Ghost sightings in the USA and around the world at the
  Haunted Places Directory on www.haunted-places.com
The Imperial Japanese Secret Weapons Museum at
  http://uk.geocities.com/sadakichi09
Microscopic views, links to articles, minutely cross-indexed,
  the Virtual Bacteria Museum at www.bacteriamuseum.org
The club rock stars are dying to get into: Tributes and
  obituaries at www.thedeadrockstarsclub.com

Acknowledgements

Many thanks to the curators who guided, corrected and encouraged me: Karen Howell, Jennifer Cornwall, D.J. Latham, Rita Schyrr, Valeria Peña, Raymond Castile, Deborah Henson-Conant, Micheal A. Hudson, Dawn Bodrogi, Claire McLean, 'Angry Johnny', Sabine Mäuseler, M.V. Moorhead, Fanny Estela, Leányvári Emöke, Melitta Franceschini, Linda Lindquist, John T. Martin, Amanda Abrell, Roger Welsch, Esther Prior, Alexis Hyman, Trey White, Mattie Faint, Lynne Belluscio, Alice League, Orin Friesen, Bill and Ann Rivers, Lee Ann Shearer, Rallou Gromitsari-Evaggelinou, Jill Schimpff, Barry Levenson, Vincenzo Giarmoleo, Alex Boese, Masaaki Machida, Steve Friesen, Bruno de Ville d'Avray, Nurdan Drignath, Karen Kamuda, John Aidiniantz, Martial Becker, Wolfgang Hillen, John Stolarczyk, Claudia Freitag-Mair, Tom Talasz, Haidee Jackson, Anne Moore, Miklós Benkóczy, David A. Treier, Michael Bohdan, Gina Huntsinger, Teresa Jover, Joshua Foer, Marvin Yakoda, David Landau, Louise Sacco, Simon Chaplin, Harry Finley, Mary Ann Rood, Alison D'Amario, Lee-ann Wilber, P.J. Fahlèn, Sigurdur Hjartarson, Martine Morand and Jean-Jacques Achache, Ernie Jurick and Ditty Nicolaides, Brian Radam, Dr Bindeshwar Pathak, Sarah Imholte, Ed Gotwalt, Rob Knoedl, Gordon Boswell, Jody White, Susanne Schmehl, Aldo Migliorini, Paulina Ochwat and especially Pat Fish.

Also many thanks to the colleagues and friends who provided news of unsuspected museums: Anne Vaughan-Williams, Wendy French, Jill Foulston, Anton and Mira Crouch. Most particularly

I am grateful to Carrie Galbraith, Annabel Eatherley, William Helfand and Pat Fish, true connoisseurs of the unusual.

Thanks to my editor Simon Flynn for his encouragement and help and to Duncan Heath and Lucy Leonhardt at Icon Books. Thanks also to Kristina Blagojevitch for her editorial and research assistance.

I Hate the Office

Malcolm Burgess

A dark, edgy yet laugh-out-loud A to Z of the absurdities and horrors of corporate life, from the pages of London's *Metro* newspaper.

Who, when they were six years old, ever said, 'Hey, I want to spend forty years of my life wondering what value-added knowledge capital is in a size-restricted cubicle surrounded by people who watch *Bargain Hunt*'?

Office workers of the world unite!

500 Reasons Why ...

I Hate The Office

'Hilarious ... cynically examines the angst of modern office life'
XFM

'Genuinely laugh-out-loud funny'
City AM

Malcolm Burgess

What makes the 9.00–5.30 sentence quite so gruesome? Office escapee Malcolm Burgess offers a painfully hilarious A to Z of reasons why the office has become the modern byword for servitude.

From the agony of the Away Day via hot desking, office politics, romance and parties, to the sheer terror of work reunions or conference calls, Burgess vents his spleen on the working week.

Ending with the unique Corporate Bullshit Detector, *I Hate the Office* is every stressed-out worker's essential weapon in the war against the angst of modern life.

ISBN: 978 1840468 24 3 • Paperback £7.99

Forty-fied

The Good, the Sad and the Bad of Fortysomething Life

Malcolm Burgess

Is being forty the new thirty or are we all just kidding ourselves?

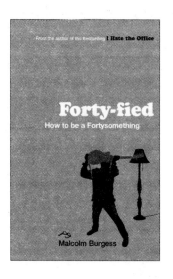

Malcolm Burgess presents a riotous A–Z of the realities of fortysomething life in the Noughties. Riotous, that is, like having your iPod on in the house. Today's fortysomethings have never had it so good – or so confusing. While our parents could look forward to a sensible middle age we're more likely to be playing our Morrissey records and thanking God Jonathan Ross is on Radio 2. There are so many different ways of being in our forties that many of us aren't quite sure where we're supposed to go next – or just how grumpy we're meant to be.

Forty-fied is the hilariously wry and observant essential guide to this complex decade in our lives. The *Metro* columnist and bestselling author of *I Hate the Office* leaves no embarrassing fortysomething scenario unturned – or do we mean unstoned?

For anyone forty and fabulous, or who's forty and owns ten fleeces, this is the laugh-out-loud funny book of your dreams ... and no doubt your screams, too.

ISBN 978 1840468 23 6 • Hardback £9.99

The Armchair Naturalist

How to be Good at Nature Without Really Trying

Johnson P. Johnson

If only everything in the countryside came with helpful name tags and instructions attached, knowing stuff about nature would be child's play. Until that day, *The Armchair Naturalist* is at hand to guide even the most urban of settlers in the ways of Britain's flora and fauna.

Teeming with illustrations, insider knowhow and shortcuts to brilliance, *The Armchair Naturalist* will transform you overnight into an expert on anything Mother Nature may throw at you, from furry animals to fir trees, cows to cowslips, blue tits to bluebells, toads to toadstools, and much more besides.

Astonish your friends as you plunge your hands into nettles without being stung. Impress even the most demanding of passing ramblers with your ability to date ancient hedgerows. Be secretly amazed at your newfound talent for predicting the weather, befriending sea birds, and knocking up a nourishing breakfast from even the most unpromising undergrowth. *The Armchair Naturalist* – your best friend in a world where half of all blackbirds are, in fact, brown.

ISBN 978 1840468 45 8 • Hardback £9.99

Wholly Irresponsible Experiments

Sean Connolly

For the little boy in every father, here's the chance to unleash the forces of nature. *Do* try these at home!

'That's the trouble with the real world. Too many people grow up. They forget. They don't remember what it's like to be twelve years old.' So said Walt Disney. How many fathers have felt that way but then just shrugged and returned to the 'real world'? How many would, deep inside, want to release the little boy inside and let rip?

Wholly Irresponsible Experiments offers a chance to do just that. Scores of experiments take you through a dazzling array of not just snaps, crackles and pops, but oozes, crashes, booms and stinks. Irresponsible – maybe. Cracking fun – definitely! Each experiment is clearly explained, with ingredients, methods, warnings and outcomes. Lively illustrations let you see what's in store.

And for those of you who still might feel a little guilty about all of this mayhem, the book includes some handy scientific 'excuses'. The child screeching across the room propelled by a fire extinguisher is, after all, demonstrating Newton's Third Law of Motion. That bit of King Edward potato launched from a tube and ricocheting around the kitchen – simple: Boyle's Law!

ISBN: 978 1840468 12 0 • Hardback £9.99

Rucks, Pucks and Sliders

More Origins of Peculiar Sporting Lingo

Bob Wilson

Would you rather deal with a falling leaf from a Monkey-hanger or God while trying to survive the Group of Death? Have you ever seen Long John or Lord Byron grab a condor with a baffing spoon from the Crow's Nest? Maybe you've sent down a slider to a flat-track bully in a baggy green and watched in delight as they became the next victim of the Slow Death?

The world of sport has its own language, wonderfully rich in strange words and phrases, whose origins often stretch back centuries. Veteran BBC presenter and football legend Bob Wilson has written this brilliant follow-up to his bestselling *Googlies, Nutmegs and Bogeys* – another illustrated guide to the fascinating true meanings, heritage and evolution of the great sporting terms we use today.

ISBN 978 1840468 25 0 • Hardback £9.99

New World Order

Dixe Wills

Nation states – you've got to have them, I suppose. But how much do we actually know about them? If you were drugged, blindfolded and parachuted into a foreign country, would you know you were in Belgium merely by picking up a handful of soil and tossing it into the air?

And nation shall rise against nation.

And the nation with most words for 'moustache' shall win.

If not, it's about time you read *New World Order*, the guide that cuts through the piffle to nail down the essence of every single country on the planet. Say goodbye to sleepless nights fretting over the average number of *puls* to the *Afghani*, or wondering what's in Bhutan today and whether it will still be fresh by the time you get it home.

With a handy grading system to reveal who are the globe's real top nations and which ones are letting the side down on a monumental scale, it's no wonder that experts are declaring *New World Order* the most important book to be written in the last 500 years. Without it, all is chaos and anarchy. And that's a bad thing apparently.

ISBN: 978 1840468 10 6 • Hardback £9.99

Hot Rods, Handguns and Huckleberry Finn

50 Facts You Need to Know: USA

Stephen Fender

The Land of the Free is the country everyone loves to attack. But how much do you really know about the USA?

Hot Rods, Handguns and Huckleberry Finn is a popular exploration of the real America.

This is a country with 50 capital cities, few of which anyone can name; a nation with 65 million gun-owners and 35,000 gun deaths each year; a place where there's one car for every adult, and where twice as many people claim to go to church as actually do.

Burning the American flag, so the Supreme Court has ruled, is now a legitimate expression of free speech. One city in Kentucky elected a black Labrador as its mayor. The US produces a quarter of all CO_2 emissions, and has a population rising twice as fast as the EU. German might have been the national language, and folk music tops the charts. Republican states especially are generous givers to charity, and they have a world-beating welfare state – the military.

Vibrant, proud and yet critical, this is a hugely enjoyable tour of the world's most powerful but least understood nation.

ISBN 978 1840468 84 7 • Paperback £10.99